GOD
at your wits' end

Other Books by Marilyn Meberg

GOD
at your wits' end

marilyn
MEBERG

W PUBLISHING GROUP
A Division of Thomas Nelson Publishers
Since 1798

www.wpublishinggroup.com

God at Your Wits' End

Unless otherwise indicated, Scripture quotations used in this book are from the *Holy Bible*, New Living Translation (NLT), copyright © 1996 by Tyndale House Publishers, Wheaton, Illinois. Used by permission.

W Publishing Group books may be purchased in bulk for educational, business, fundraising, or sales promotional use. For information, please email SpecialMarkets@ThomasNelson.com.

Other Scripture quotations are taken from the following sources:

The Holy Bible, New International Version (NIV). Copyright © 1973, 1978, 1984, International Bible Society. Used by permission of Zondervan Bible Publishers. The King James Version of the Bible (KJV). *The Message* (MSG), copyright ©1993. Used by permission of NavPress Publishing Group. New American Standard Bible (NASB), ©1960, 1977, 1995 by the Lockman Foundation. The New King James Version (NKJV®), copyright 1979, 1980, 1982, Thomas Nelson, Inc., Publishers.

Names and details in some anecdotes and illustrations have been changed to protect identities.

Library of Congress Cataloging-in-Publication Data available

Printed in the United States of America
05 06 07 08 09 QWM 9 8 7 6 5 4 3 2 1

Contents

Introduction

The good news
about being at your wits' end

*They reel to and fro, and . . . are at their wits' end. Then they
cry out to the LORD in their trouble, and He brings them out
of their distresses.*

—Psalm 107:27–28 NKJV

To be human is to spend some time at our "wits' end," perhaps reeling to and fro. Most of us have expended time and
energy trying to find solutions to our various wits'-end dilemmas. Sometimes we use problem-solving skills that seem sensible to us, and in so doing we may see our circumstances change
for the better. When that happens, we sigh with relief that yet
another crisis has been averted. We may even feel pleased that
we managed the crisis on our own and didn't have to bother
God with it. He has enough problems without our becoming
a continual burden to Him. Surely, we think, He means for us
to figure out a few things on our own.

But what if we *can't* figure these things out on our own? What
if, at our wits' end, we feel lost in pain, confusion, desperation,
and fear? Those are the kinds of emotions that drive us to "cry
out to the LORD" in our trouble. To be at our wits' end is,
according to *Webster's*, "to have [your] back against the wall."

The good news is, when our backs are against the wall—when
we cry out to the Lord—He is there. God is always at our wits'

end. How do we know? Because God is wherever we are. His promise is to never, ever leave us. Wherever we may wander, in foolishness or fear, God does not leave us.

That astounding truth is accompanied by yet another astounding truth found in our scriptural theme passage, Psalm 107:27–28: when we cry out to the Lord, He brings us out of our distresses. Why does God do that? The answer is repeatedly stated throughout the entire chapter of Psalm 118 (NIV). He does it because "his love endures forever." In spite of our mindless wandering that may produce wits'-end dilemmas, "his love endures forever."

It's an awesome promise but one that is difficult for many of us to incorporate into our daily living. For some reason, its truth is beyond our grasp. We may believe God's love endures forever in some sort of mystical, far-from-us way, but if the whole truth were known, it does not seem real for our nitty-gritty reality.

So what's the problem? Why can't we "get it"—that when we call out in our distresses He will bring us out of our troubles? Why can't we simply settle into the biblical drumbeat message that God's love endures forever?

I think the problem lies in the contrast between what we believe and what we think. In our hearts we *believe* that God's love endures forever, but in our heads we sometimes *think* in a way that creates roadblocks to faith. For example, our faulty thinking might lead us to have questions like these:

- If He loves me so much, why do I hurt so much?

- Am I being punished? I thought I was forgiven.

- Who's in charge of my life? Can I trust that answer?
- Why is faith so hard? What if I don't have enough?

Faulty thinking leads to shaky faith, and shaky faith can put your back against the wall. This book is about how you can find your way to a faith that is practical and within your grasp, and how you can eliminate the faulty thinking that keeps you at your wits' end. Each chapter addresses a common question produced by faulty thinking and then shows you how to get past the roadblock and find your way to a faith that endures.

The God who is always there cares even more about your quest for faith than you do. His intent is to meet you where you are in your faith need and to lovingly show you what it means when He tells you He will bring you out of your distresses. That's what this book is all about.

Faulty Thought No. 1:
I need a sign

Several years ago when our baby Joani was born with spina bifida, the prognosis for her surviving was poor. I loved and trusted our pastor, but as we moved through those stressful days wracked with sorrow and fear, I wanted to ask some theological questions in total anonymity. I didn't want my pastor to know my faith had been shaken to the core by Joani's condition, so I made an appointment with a local pastor whom I did not know but whose ministry I had observed and thought I trusted.

After I briefed him on our situation, the pastor leaned across his desk and said, "Marilyn, could there be any unconfessed sin in your life? Could there be any in Ken's life?"

Shocked by his question, my faltering response was, "Are you suggesting Joani was born with spina bifida because of our possible sin?"

His answer was for us to do a thorough soul-search and confess everything displeasing to God. I asked him if, once that gargantuan task was completed, Joani would be healed.

His answer was, "Take it to the Lord."

I was devastated when I walked into that pastor's office, but I was doubly devastated when I walked out. Could it be that some sins had gotten past me and were never confessed? Could it be that my sin or Ken's sin had resulted in an innocent child's being born with a crippling disability? Was Joani's condition a sign that God was punishing us for our lack of righteousness?

It took me some time to work out all that faulty thinking, and I'll share more about why it *is* faulty in the next chapter. I finally realized if that pastor's assumptions were true, the entire world would be on crutches, because *no one* is born to totally sinless parents!

It's frightening to realize how faulty thinking can alter our belief systems and erode our faith. It's also disturbing to see that even church leaders can develop and promote faulty thoughts that impede our faith rather than strengthen it.

To sort through the thoughts that crowd our minds during times of stress and heartache, we need a sound scriptural foundation, a heart of faith, and a "discerning mind," the kind of mind David asked God to give him as He had promised to do (see Psalm 119:169). And we need to remember the teaching of Proverbs 3:5, which says to "trust in the LORD with all your heart; do not depend on your own understanding."

Misunderstanding Who God Is

My "own understanding" can be full of faulty thinking, which leads me away from developing a scriptural belief system that leads to a firm faith. Faulty thinking comes from a misunderstanding of who God is. You may remember that when Job was being tested seemingly beyond human endurance, one of his "comforters" suggested Job's calamities must have come upon him as a result of his sin. When God ultimately restored Job to health and prosperity,

He turned to the "comforters" and said, "I am angry with you . . . for you have not been right in what you said about me" (Job 42:7).

Faulty thinking comes from a misunderstanding of who God is.

We want to have an accurate understanding of God. When great difficulties beset us—when a child dies, a job is lost, a marriage fails, or some other calamity occurs—we long for reassurance that "his love endures forever" (Psalm 118:1 NIV) and that He is actively working for good in our lives. We want to believe He's hearing us when we cry out to Him in our distresses.

But when we're in a faulty-thinking mind-set, we think we need a tangible, visible sign that these promises are true. Perhaps we seek the kind of miraculous sign Moses used to convince the people of Israel that God had, indeed, sent him to lead them out of bondage. When God told Moses to tell the Israelites they were going to be delivered, Moses argued with God:

"Look, they won't believe me! They won't do what I tell them. They'll just say, 'The LORD never appeared to you.'"

Then the LORD asked him, "What do you have there in your hand?"

"A shepherd's staff," Moses replied.

"Throw it down on the ground," the LORD told him. So Moses threw it down, and it became a snake! Moses was terrified, so he turned and ran away.

But when God told him to grab the snake by its tail, he obeyed—and the snake became a shepherd's staff again. God wrapped up the conversation by saying, "Perform this sign, and they will believe you" (see Exodus 4:1–5).

In those Old Testament times, the rod that went from being a shepherd's staff to a snake and back again prompted belief among the Israelites because it was observable and tangible. Faulty thinking tells us we need that same kind of sign today. And when it doesn't come—when there's no visible, emotional, or tangible evidence of His working things out in our lives, answering our prayers the way we want Him to and within the time frame we want Him to—we may sink into the dirt of discouragement.

> *Faith is believing what we can't see, what is not tangible, and in some cases, does not make sense.*

To get past this pit of faulty thinking, we need to understand the difference between *belief* and *faith*. Though similar, the two have an important difference. The dictionary defines *belief* as "mental acceptance of or conviction in the truth or actuality of something." In contrast, *faith* goes beyond mental acceptance. Faith is believing what we can't see, what is not tangible, and in some cases, does not make sense. The dictionary states that "faith does not rest on logical proof or material evidence." Sounds right in line with the biblical definition of faith in Hebrews 11:1: "the confident assurance that what we hope for is going to happen. It is the evidence of things we cannot yet see."

God's Gracious Gift

While we may not have miraculous "signs" that provide this kind of evidence of God's enduring love, we are fortunate today that God graciously provides another type of gift to help keep our faith strong. I call this gift a *faith object,* and there's no better way to illustrate it than through the athletic prowess of the Hedrick Racing Pigs.

OK, I'll explain. The Hedrick Racing Pigs are fast-paced porkers who hurtle down a racetrack for the competition's only prize . . . an Oreo cookie. I learned of them several weeks ago, when my attention was captured by the newspaper headline "Racing Pigs Run for the Love of a Cookie." Of course that appealed to my quirky nature, so I read on. I learned there are twelve pigs who make up the Hedrick Exotic Animal pig-racing team. They run, not for honor or even for the thrill of victory, but for the coveted prize of one Oreo cookie. Tim Hart, their trainer, says the pigs endure two to three weeks of rigorous training before they qualify for competition. He pointed out that his pigs are not the usual stick 'em in a pen, fatten 'em up, and then see 'em off to market types. They are all lean, eager pigs with one goal in mind: that Oreo cookie.

Now, let's suppose that one day before a race the four pig stars, Jean Claude Van Ham, Sylvester Staloin, Arnold Snoutzenhogger, and Rush Limhog (I did not make up those names; they were in the newspaper), were feeling a bit disgruntled and did not want to race. Their reason? They had not actually seen a cookie in weeks. They no longer had the visual assurance that there truly was a cookie at the end of the racetrack, and as a result they had lost their belief that it was even there. (Actually, they had not seen a cookie because for weeks another pig racer, Snoop Hoggy Hog, had gotten to the finish line first, snatched the cookie, and devoured it on the spot.) Thus the four other competitors now sank to the dirt in discouragement, their belief system destroyed, their racing days perhaps over. They had to come to their wits' end.

For the racing pigs, the Oreo served as a *faith object,* a tangible object that helped them believe in what they could not actually see. A faith object is something that can be seen, experienced, and remembered. When the pigs remembered that the Oreo was waiting for them at the finish line, they ran their little hearts out, trotting eagerly toward the goal. But the longer the loser pigs went without seeing the Oreo, the weaker their belief was that it actually existed. And finally, they just lay down and gave up.

> *In order to have faith, I must move beyond*
> *mental acceptance. In faith I hold fast to something,*
> *or rather, to Someone, whom I cannot see.*
> *And that Someone is Jesus.*

I hate to tell you how easily I understand the discouragement of Arnold Snoutzenhogger and his other three racing buddies. For one thing, both the pigs and I live in expectation of a reward. When I do a good thing, like winning a race (not that I've experienced exactly *that* specific "good thing" in more than half a century), I want praise, recognition, or at least an Oreo. Sure, I'd like to think I would run the race of life based on faith and not on the vision of tangible rewards. But all too often I slip into the faulty thinking that says I *do* need a sign—a piece of visual, emotional, or tangible evidence that God is aware of my struggles and is hearing my cries for help.

When this happens, I ask myself, *Marilyn, is this discouragement you're feeling due to shaky faith or faulty thinking?* I have to remind myself that in order to have faith, I must move *beyond* mental acceptance. In faith I hold fast to something, or rather, to Someone, whom I cannot see. And that Someone is Jesus.

Experiencing Salvation . . . Because of a Turtle

I came to know Jesus through a rather unorthodox route— a reptile. Were it not for the life and death of Leroy Walker, I might never have experienced salvation. Leroy came into and out of my life when I was five years old. Leroy was my turtle. He probably would have lived a long and productive life had our neighbor lady not restricted him from her garden. He'd apparently wandered into her lettuce patch one afternoon and was wreaking havoc. When I was introduced to Leroy, she suggested he could be my pet if I just kept him off her property.

Unfortunately, the food I provided Leroy wasn't sufficiently palatable; he soon succumbed to the "failure to thrive" syndrome. For several reasons I was stricken by his death. For one, I had envisioned great companionable walks for the two of us, even though the string-leash I managed to get around his neck obviously annoyed him. He pulled into his shell and stayed there until I disappeared from view.

In addition to grieving his death, I felt a sudden fear of my own death. I'd overheard my father tell my mother he'd be surprised if I lived to be six. (I was constantly flinging myself off anything over ten feet high. I felt sure I'd be able to fly if I could just get my arm rhythm right.) Leroy's death occurred shortly before my sixth birthday.

Hearing my concerns, my mother gently coached me in how to receive Jesus into my heart. I prayed immediately, stumbling over a five-year-old's version of the sinner's prayer—something like, "Dear Jesus, I believe You are God's only Son and that You died on the cross and arose from the dead, and I hope You will forgive me for my sins and take me to heaven when I die so I can live with You forever and ever. Amen."

Mother assured me that should my untimely death occur, I would instantly be in heaven, a place that was perfect and where no one died. What a tremendous relief that was for my young, anxious heart!

Looking back, I don't think my conversion was a faith-motivated experience; it was more from fear than anything. I didn't have a clue what real faith is. The faith I did have was in my mother, who explained salvation to me. It made sense that God loved me (I saw no reason then why He shouldn't), and I liked the idea of Jesus living within me forever. All in all, it sounded like a good deal.

To combat faulty thinking, we need a firm, utterly reliable faith object, and we have one. It's the Bible.

Salvation still sounds like a good deal; in fact, it *is* a good deal. For me, conversion was simple because my faith object was my mother. I trusted her; she was reliable and she was also tangible. I could see her and hear her voice. She said there is a God who loves me, and His Son, Jesus, forgives sin (the sin thing made perfect sense to me), and with His forgiveness I would one day follow Leroy Walker into eternity. (The Leroy part was my idea.) I had faith in the whole transaction because I had faith in my mother.

We may think we need Old Testament–style "signs" (although I'm not sure I would want a shepherd's staff that turns into a snake) in order to have faith, but that's faulty thinking. Instead, God very graciously provides faith objects to encourage our continued and future faith. They help us believe in what we cannot imagine to be true. To combat faulty thinking, we need a firm, utterly reliable faith object, and we have one. It's the Bible. It's tangible, I can see it, I always have access to it, and I have faith in what it says.

In the next chapter I'm going to discuss how the Bible keeps our thinking straight and our faith grounded. Many Christians have faulty thinking on the subject of how past sin determines the events of their lives. They go through life bent over with guilt and regret thinking God must be punishing them for their sin even though it was confessed and forgiven. "How else," they ask, "can we explain the hurt in our lives?"

What does the Bible have to say on that subject? We need to know. It's crucial for the building of our faith.

1. Belief is mental acceptance. One can believe in God, mentally accept that He is, but still not have faith in Him. Faith goes beyond mental acceptance to the place of having faith in what is not seen. In which of the two categories do you most frequently find yourself?

2. How does it help you to understand the two categories?

3. In what ways do you recognize faulty thinking in your approach to God? Can you describe some faulty thinking that has influenced your decisions?

Faulty Thought No. 2:

It must be my fault

When Jesus healed a man who had been blind from birth, His disciples asked, "Teacher, why was this man born blind? Was it a result of his own sins or those of his parents?"

"It was not because of his sins or his parents' sins," Jesus answered. "He was born blind so the power of God could be seen in him" (see John 9:1–3).

In spite of Jesus's clearly telling the disciples the blind man's condition was not because of sin, they seemed hesitant to accept that answer. Why?

It was common Old Testament thinking to believe that when bad things happened to someone it was punishment for sin. In the previous chapter we discussed how Job's "comforters" thought Job must have committed some whopper sin to bring on all the losses he experienced. That assumption made God cranky. Jesus too was abrupt with the disciples when they questioned the origin of the man's blindness. The disciples were obviously convinced that sin was the problem; they just wanted to know *whose* sin brought it on. Jesus derailed their thinking when He told them no one's sin caused the man's blindness.

A Whole New Order

So why did the disciples think suffering and physical impairment were the result of sin? And why did Job's friends share the same assumption? The reality is, the Old Testament supported those assumptions. For example, Jeremiah 17:10 (NASB) says, "I, the LORD, search the heart, I test the mind, even to give to each man according to his ways, according to the results of his deeds." I wouldn't call that a particularly comforting verse! In fact, it sounds like I'm gonna get it, based on the results of my deeds!

Isaiah 13:11 (NASB) isn't any more comforting: "I will punish the world for its evil and the wicked for their iniquity." Then there's the Isaiah 57:21 reminder that "there is no peace for the wicked."

Mercy! I need a cup of tea.

But I can set my teacup down because the comforting news is that those verses describe the person whose sins have not yet been paid for by Jesus. Scripture gives us a frighteningly clear picture of how, if we are given what we deserve based on the results of our deeds, we're all in trouble. Yes, sin and evil produce no peace for the wicked.

The disciples did not yet get the picture that "as many as believed on [Jesus] would not perish" and "by [Jesus's] stripes we are healed" (Isaiah 53:5 NKJV). Until Jesus, the world lived in condemnation. The only way out of that condemnation was to live purely and perfectly. The way to live purely and perfectly was to conscientiously follow the commandments and then to participate in the animal sacrifices for sin when one messed up somewhere in trying to keep every single one of the commandments.

You are not paying for your sin right now as you read these words. Your sin has already been paid for.

With Jesus came a whole new order of things. We are no longer held accountable for the perfection we could never achieve or for the good works we could never accomplish, because Jesus rescued us from the sinful limitations of our humanity. Ephesians 2:8–10 nutshells the new way for us:

> God saved you by his special favor when you believed. And you can't take credit for this; it is a gift from God. Salvation is not a reward for the good things we have done, so none of us can boast about it. For we are God's masterpiece. He has created us anew in Christ Jesus, so that we can do the good things he planned for us long ago.

Old Testament thinking was, You get what you deserve if you sin. The disciples and Job's comforters were thinking in the old way. Jesus came to show His creation that a new way is possible because He died for sin. The result is, you don't pay for your sin. Jesus paid for it. You may have sinned a whopper, but you don't ever have to crawl up on the cross. With that incredible truth comes this additional amazing fact: You are not paying for your sin right now as you read these words. Your sin has already been paid for. It's a done deal.

Payment Versus Consequences

You may, however, be paying the consequences of your sin. Many people confuse payment for sin and consequence of sin. Jeremiah 31:34 says, "I will forgive their wickedness and will never again remember their sins." The problem is, *we* remember our sins because we may have to live with the daily consequences.

For example, we had a neighbor who was convicted on several counts of business fraud. He is a Christian and was knowingly sinning until he was caught, tried, and sent to a penitentiary. He confessed his sin and God forgave him, but he still is paying the consequences. He will, in fact, be paying for eight more years.

In spite of the biblical assurance that in Jesus we are new creations and there is no condemnation because we are in Him, many persons persist in the faulty thinking that God is punishing them for their sins.

Mr. Davidson was a peculiarly crotchety old man who was a member of the church my dad pastored. Mr. Davidson gave me the fantods because his constant response to anyone experiencing difficulty was, "Must be sin in your life." I was an inordinately sensitive little kid, so I avoided him as much as possible. I knew something in my behavior would be interpreted by him as "sin in my life," and I feared he might know something I didn't.

During an Easter Communion service, I, at the age of seven, exhibited a depth-perception problem in trying to replace my Communion cup in the slotted tray that was passed up and down the pews. I overshot the tiny hole in which the cup was to be placed, causing it to drop to the floor, where it shattered, prompting Mr. Davidson to mutter, "sin in her life."

Mr. Davidson's favorite verse was Exodus 32:34 (NASB): "In the day when I punish, I will punish them for their sin." I can still see Mr. Davidson waggling his arthritic finger as he commonly did during the tiny testimony-and-prayer service on Wednesday nights. I always felt he waggled it at me.

Though Mr. Davidson was admittedly an odd duck, there are still way too many Mr. Davidsons waggling fingers in eager judgment. They thrive on verses like Isaiah 40:23: "He judges the great people of the world and brings them all to nothing," or Deuteronomy 7:10–11: "[God] does not hesitate to punish and destroy those who hate him. Therefore, obey all these commands, laws, and regulations I am giving you today."

Perhaps it is not just Mr. Davidson and his type who need to understand the context of those verses that sound as if we're doomed before our first cup of tea each morning. Let's take a quick refresher course on how to bring together these two biblical viewpoints. It will help eliminate some of our faulty thinking.

Divine Enablement

You will remember God made a gigantic promise to Abraham to provide innumerable heirs and descendants. That promise was called a covenant, which is an agreement. God said to Abraham, "I will establish My covenant between Me and you and your descendants after you throughout their generations for an everlasting covenant" (Genesis 17:7 NASB).

Then, when God met with Moses at Sinai and gave him the Ten Commandments, God said, "Now if you will obey me and keep my covenant, you will be my own special treasure from among all the nations of the earth; for all the earth belongs to me" (Exodus 19:5).

At first, that sounded good to the people. They knew exactly what God expected of them. They had a set of rules, and all they had to do was follow them. Some of the people were able to follow the rules because they weren't inclined to murder, rob, or sleep with their neighbors anyway. But all the people found it impossible to keep from breaking the rules having to do with their minds, perhaps thinking thoughts such as, *I can stay out of my neighbor's bed, but I can't keep her out of my head. I can keep myself from stealing my neighbor's kinnor, but I can't help coveting it.* (Sorry. I had to throw that in when I found out a kinnor had ten strings that were tuned pentatonically without semitones. Mercy! If I can't have semitones in order to tune pentatonically, I don't even want a kinnor!)

So what happened when the people found it impossible to always obey and keep God's commandments? God made a new covenant with His people. *He* knew they could not live according to the old covenant, but *they* needed to know that too. So the new covenant held a provision that would enable the people to live a life of the obedience God required. Without it they would live continuously at their wits' end.

> *The new covenant promised divine enablement.*
> *It promised the Spirit of God would literally be poured*
> *into the hearts of His people, giving them*
> *power to obey.*

The new covenant is recorded in Jeremiah 31:33: "I will put my laws in their minds, and I will write them on their hearts. I will be their God, and they will be my people."

I love the way that same covenant is expressed in Ezekiel 36:25–27 because it specifies even more hope for the failing rule keeper:

I will sprinkle clean water on you, and you will be clean. Your filth will be washed away, and you will no longer worship idols. And I will give you a new heart with new and right desires, and I will put a new spirit in you. I will take out your stony heart of sin and give you a new, obedient heart. And I will put my Spirit in you so you will obey my laws and do whatever I command.

This is more encouraging. In contrast to the old covenant, in which there was no power to obey God's law, the new covenant promised divine enablement. It promised the Spirit of God would literally be poured into the hearts of His people, giving them power to obey. When they were at their wits' end, God brought them out of their distresses with this new covenant.

Victory as Well as Salvation

This second covenant points to the future role of Jesus, not only for salvation, but for victory. It is clearly stated in Romans 8:1–4:

So now there is no condemnation for those who belong to Christ Jesus. For the power of the life-giving Spirit has freed you through Christ Jesus from the power of sin that leads to death. The law of Moses could not save us, because of our sinful nature. But God put into effect a different plan to save us. He sent his own Son in a human body like ours, except that ours are sinful. God destroyed sin's control over us by giving his

Son as a sacrifice for our sins. He did this so that the requirement of the law would be fully accomplished for us who no longer follow our sinful nature but instead follow the Spirit.

How's that for great news? You and I can't keep God's laws. Not keeping God's laws is sin. The wages of sin is death. Jesus died for that sin. We are not condemned for what we can't do. Mr. Davidson liked to say, "God will punish them for their sins." Jesus says, "Not over My dead and risen body"!

Let's go back now to that rather shocking scene from chapter 1 and more fully explore the question asked of me when I sought counsel about Joani's spina bifida. Was her physical challenge brought upon her because of the "sins of the parents"? There was no doubt there was sin in our lives; to live in the human condition is to live with sins such as envy, jealousy, impatience, self-sufficiency, etc. (And I am not minimizing the "etc." of our sins.) But were I to be condemned for my humanity, I would no longer live in the grace of God, who declares me perfect because of Jesus. I would instead live under the law and with utter self-absorption continually scrutinize my life for ungodly thinking and behavior.

Therefore, I do not think our sins produced Joani's spina bifida, but there is no doubt that sin *was* its root cause. What sin was that? The sin that cracked the perfection of the Garden of Eden. There, the choice by shortsighted, self-serving narcissists to disobey the God of the universe with a finger-waggling defiance produced forever after an imperfect world dominated by a sin impulse.

We need to know the incredible consequence of the fall of humankind in the Garden of Eden. We need to know that the price paid for sin was the death of Jesus, and without that act we would continually be making Old Testament–style animal sacrifices for our sins in order to be forgiven.

Refocusing from the Why to the How

Now, knowing sin's price has been paid and knowing we need no longer assume we are being punished, we move away from the sin-cause into a new way of thinking about the *why* behind the events of our lives. Let's look again at the story of the blind man.

Jesus's response to the disciples' questions about the root cause of the man's blindness is interesting because the cause is not even addressed. Jesus didn't explain what caused the man's physical imperfections. He merely said, "He was born blind so the power of God could be seen in him." This can be a troubling implication: Did God cause the blindness for His own ultimate glory? Most commentators agree that God is not accused of causing the condition but that the blind man's condition can be viewed as a way to glorify God. Similarly, in my life I have a choice in how to think about Joani's condition. I can fruitlessly search for the *why* of her brief little life, or I can change my focus and consider how God can be glorified as a result of her life.

Jesus did not explain the why of the blind man's suffering. Neither did God explain the why of Job's suffering. Both Father and Son focused not on what happened or why but on the *what is*. The lesson we learn from these examples is that knowing the *why* is not as important as our response to the *what is*.

> *I want to leave the battlefield and focus on*
> *the ultimate victory that always comes with siding*
> *with God. The battle isn't mine; it's God's,*
> *and He has already won.*

Actually, that is a liberating approach to the problem of pain. We can certainly say with biblical support that we live in a battlefield in which there is a constant struggle between the forces of good and evil: God and Satan. This understanding partially explains the why, but it isn't satisfying because there is no forward movement in that thinking. I can get stuck there. I want to leave the battlefield and focus on the ultimate victory that always comes with siding with God. The battle isn't mine; it's God's, and He has already won. I want to celebrate that victory, and I want to experience all things working together for good (see Romans 8:28). I'll miss it if my focus is only human and preoccupied with the why.

I think God was cranky with Job's friends because their focus was wrong. From their example we learn that the issue is whether we will maintain our faith when we don't understand what's going on. Job didn't get it at first, and neither did the disciples. Quite frankly, sometimes I don't get it either. (I'm going to tell you about one of those "I don't get it" times in a later chapter.)

But this is what I *do* get: I live in a world dominated by the consequences of the original sin-choice. That means there will always be spina bifida, cancer, and other heart-wrenching body assaults. Living in this world means people will kill one another, rape one another, and rob one another. It means some people will die too young, and others will live too long.

But living in this world also means I have a warrior Savior who died for all that sin surrounding me, and I need not be its victim. I need not succumb to faulty thinking and feel I'm being punished. Instead, I choose to believe and have faith like David's when he wrote:

> *Though I walk in the midst of trouble, You will revive me;*
> *You will stretch forth Your hand against the wrath of*
> *   my enemies,*
> *And Your right hand will save me.*
> *The LORD will accomplish what concerns me;*
> *Your lovingkindness, O LORD, is everlasting.*
> *(Psalm 138:7–8 NASB)*

People may think, *Well, then, if I'm not being punished for my sin, maybe it all boils down to the possibility that God really isn't all that crazy about me. There must be something wrong with me, because my life is not going all that well. Maybe what's wrong is simply that God doesn't like me much.*

That's the faulty thinking we'll examine in the next chapter.

1. Name one sin for which it is hard to believe you are not being punished. Do you recognize any faulty thinking? If so, what is it?

2. Does knowing God is not punishing you affect how you feel about Him? How?

3. Why do you suppose God did not explain the "why" of Job's suffering? Why did Jesus not explain the "why" of suffering?

4. What does the Psalm 138:8 phrase "The LORD will accomplish what concerns me" mean to you? How has it worked in your life?

Faulty Thought No. 3:
God doesn't like me much

Buford Thomas was a man who lived in the same community as crotchety old Mr. Davidson, the gnarled naysayer who shot "must be sin in your life" bullets at everyone. Though Buford lived in our church community, he never attended church. He told my dad many times, "Parson, it don't do no good you telling me God loves me. I know different. There's just somethin' about me He don't cotton to."

Buford's negative insistence illustrates another faulty-thinking position that erodes the growth potential for faith. It's the sneaking suspicion that God does not really like us much. In spite of our understanding of the "God is love" declaration we read in 1 John 4:16 and in many other passages of Scripture, we are quietly unconvinced. I say *quietly* because the fact of God's loving us is such a basic and primary teaching, we'd hate to admit we're stuck there and can't seem to move beyond it. But if the truth were known, many of us would have to say, with Buford, "There's just something about me God does not take to."

Buford had a farm outside of town. (I'm not sure if a population of 102 qualifies for the designation of "town," but I'll label the little community as such.) My father was one of ten kids raised on a farm in eastern Canada, so Dad knew and understood farming. He would often go over to Buford's and help with various farming chores. Dad loved doing it, but he also wanted to be a human representative of God's love for Buford.

One day after successfully but frantically getting the recently cut hay into Buford's barn before the inevitable rain hit, Buford and Dad sat down with a cup of way-too-strong coffee. As they luxuriated in their victory of beating the rain, Buford turned to Dad and said, "Ya know, Parson, I really like you. And I know you like me. But ya gotta know, just 'cause *you* do don't mean God does. There's just somethin' about me He don't cotton to."

Now, admittedly, Buford was an uneducated man who perhaps lacked intellectual capacity. But I've met many well-educated and intellectual persons who firmly believe they seem to possess some repellent quality that causes God to simply not "cotton to" them.

One such guy nearly fell out of his tree when Jesus extended His love to him. You remember Zacchaeus, the short little tax collector we read about in Luke 19. When the news spread that Jesus was going to be passing through Jericho, Zacchaeus was determined to catch at least a glimpse of Him, so he climbed a tree to ensure a good view. To the astonishment of everyone, including Zacchaeus, Jesus stopped under Zacchaeus's tree, looked up at him, and said, "Come down immediately. I must stay at your house today" (v. 5 NIV).

Now, Zacchaeus possessed a number of unique, repellent qualities that he could have assumed would cause Jesus not to cotton to him. Zacchaeus was short. That is hardly a repellent quality, but Zacchaeus may have considered it to be a unique negative. Some people think being short is a disadvantage; they think tall people make a positive statement, appearing more confident, self-assured, and capable. We don't know that Zacchaeus had a little-man complex, but I wonder if it wasn't hard on his ego to have to climb a tree to see what was going on. I also wonder if it was embarrassing when Jesus stopped dead in His tracks, looked up at the tree sitter, and told him to climb back down. A large crowd witnessed this event, and that crowd hated Zacchaeus. Jesus blew his cover.

Zacchaeus was hated by the people for understandable reasons. He was repellent because he was a tax collector. You will remember the Jews were living under the political domination of the Roman Empire at that time. In the Roman Empire, bids were taken for the right to collect taxes in a given region. Those who won the bid were required to pay a set amount to Rome, but anything they collected above that amount they could keep.

Zacchaeus overcharged his fellow Jews in the region of Judea and pocketed the difference. As a result, he was a very rich man. It was utterly repellent behavior for Zacchaeus to profit from his own people. They knew it, he knew it, and Jesus knew it. One would think God would not cotton to that kind of guy. We might assume Zacchaeus thought that too.

Scumbag Conversions

Interestingly enough, Jesus cottoned to another tax collector as well as to Zacchaeus. His name was Matthew. When Jesus saw Matthew sitting at his tax collector's booth one day and said simply, "Come, be My disciple," Matthew promptly left his booth and lucrative career to follow Jesus.

We read in Matthew's Gospel that Matthew had what could be described as a scum party the evening of his calling to be a disciple of Jesus. How would you get invited to a scum party?

You would qualify if you were a robber, murderer, or tax collector. They were all lumped together as scum, these social outcasts. Matthew described that dinner party in Matthew 9:10–13:

> That night Matthew invited Jesus and his disciples to be his dinner guests, along with his fellow tax collectors and many other notorious sinners. The Pharisees were indignant. "Why does your teacher eat with such scum?" they asked his disciples. When he heard this, Jesus replied, "Healthy people don't need a doctor—sick people do." Then he added, ". . . For I have come to call sinners, not those who think they are already good enough."

Matthew could not have thought he was good enough to be a disciple of Jesus. Zacchaeus could not have thought he was good enough to provide hospitality for Jesus. But Jesus chose them. Why? Because they were sinners; because they needed a divine doctor. Jesus cottoned to sinners, not because of their sinful behavior, but because He wanted to offer a cure for the sin that produced the behavior. One didn't have to appear acceptable to get the attention and healing focus of God's Son, Jesus. One had to be imperfect: a sinner.

From a human perspective, we find it amazing that Matthew became a devoted follower of Jesus, who trusted Matthew and considered him worthy of his position. Matthew has the distinct honor of having written his eyewitness account of Jesus's public ministry. His account was chosen to be the first book of the New Testament. This was the divinely inspired work of he who was considered scum before he met Jesus.

Perhaps the most well-known scumbag conversion was that of the thief on the cross. He was being crucified because of his repellent lack of morality. His unacceptable, unlawful behavior condemned him to the most horrifically brutal punishment ever decreed. But something happened to him on the cross that went far beyond the physical agony he was experiencing. He wasn't in denial of his own guilt. He accepted the reality that he was indeed guilty as charged. The account in Luke 23:35–41 reads,

The crowd watched, and the leaders laughed and scoffed. "He saved others," they said, "let him save himself if he is really God's Chosen One, the Messiah." The soldiers mocked him, too, by offering him a drink of sour wine. They called out to him, "If you are the King of the Jews, save yourself!" A signboard was nailed to the cross above him with these words: "This is the King of the Jews."

One of the criminals hanging beside him scoffed, "So you're the Messiah, are you? Prove it by saving yourself—and us, too, while you're at it!"

But the other criminal protested, "Don't you fear God even when you are dying? We deserve to die for our evil deeds, but this man hasn't done anything wrong."

This is an amazing declaration of belief. The thief must have known of Jesus. He must have been aware of His many compassionate acts and miracles. But more important, the thief had an "aha!" moment when he realized Jesus was not only an innocent man hanging unjustly between two criminals, He was who He said He was. He was the King of the Jews. At this point the thief had a belief, a mental assent, but he had to act on what he had come to believe. He did that with his request: "Jesus, remember me when you come into your Kingdom" (v. 42).

That symbolic coming forward was all it took for Jesus to respond with the words "I assure you, today you will be with me in paradise" (v. 43). The hanging, dying criminal had every reason to think he would be one God wouldn't cotton to. And yet, as with Zacchaeus, Matthew, and countless others, Jesus did what God the Father sent Him to do, and that was to continue to love, heal, and provide salvation for His fractured creation.

Now let's look at the crucifixion scene we've just discussed from Jesus's perspective. He had, prior to being hung on the cross by huge nails pounded through His hands, been brutally beaten. The Roman method of pre-crucifixion punishment was to administer blow after blow to the bared back using a lash intertwined with pieces of bone or steel. These beatings themselves were often sufficiently brutal to cause death. If he survived the beating, the prisoner was then nailed to a cross. Commentators point out that the excruciating pain that came from being suspended by two nailed hands caused the blood to sink rapidly into the lower extremities of the body. Within six to twelve minutes, the blood pressure would drop to half while the rate of the pulse would double. The heart would be deprived of blood, and fainting would follow. Death during crucifixion was usually due to heart failure.

Would you not think if ever there were a time when Jesus could tend to His own agony without having to think of the needs of others, it would be as He hung on the cross? Would you not think that in the midst of the demeaning taunts and ridicule hurled upon Him by the demonic persons delighting in His torture that Jesus had earned the right to say, "I've given everything I have for you, so you can simply be assured the fires of hell will one day consume you. I'm finished with you!"?

No, anything but those human thoughts were in the mind of Christ. Instead, He said, "Father, forgive them; for they do not know what they are doing" (Luke 23:34 NASB). Jesus came to earth "to seek and save those . . . who are lost" (Luke 19:10), and He continued His mission of saving even from the cross as He compassionately assured the criminal of his place in paradise.

This gracious assurance of salvation to the thief gives evidence that the Savior never turns away from us when we reach out to Him. He was not preoccupied with His own need on the cross.

His heart is always tuned to the needs of His creation. Our cries for help are always heard. In addition to that good news, there's no sin He cannot or will not forgive. There are no good deeds we must first perform in order to be good enough for salvation. The thief brought nothing to Jesus but his splattered record of sin. Immediately the thief was forgiven; immediately the thief was worthy to join Jesus in paradise.

Listen to these prophetic words from Isaiah 1:18 that promise forgiveness for all sin: "No matter how deep the stain of your sins, I can remove it. I can make you as clean as freshly fallen snow. Even if you are stained as red as crimson, I can make you as white as wool."

What motivates these promises of forgiveness? What motivates Jesus's selection of those who are imperfect? What motivates Jesus to put aside His own agony and focus on the request of a man who was scum before he met Jesus on the cross? The answer reverberates and fills the entire universe; it is the love of God for those whom He created to receive that love.

If we persist in thinking there's just something about us that God does not cotton to, we would have to rewrite the Bible to prove it! There is instead just something about us He is crazy about! To think otherwise is faulty thinking. To think otherwise is to have no faith in our faith object, the Word of God, which tells us just how strong is His love for us.

Romans 8:38–39 describes the strength of that love:

> I am convinced that nothing can ever separate us from his love. Death can't, and life can't. . . . Our fears for today, our worries about tomorrow, and even the powers of hell can't keep God's love away. Whether we are high above the sky or in the deepest ocean, nothing in all creation will ever be able to separate us from the love of God that is revealed in Christ Jesus our Lord.

Buford finally realized God did, indeed, cotton to him after all. He also came to understand nothing could take that "cottoning-to" love away from him. Here's how it happened.

Buford never married; he lived with his beloved and smelly dog, Chester. They were inseparable; that meant Buford was also smelly. (That fact, of course, has nothing to do with anything.)

One morning Buford and Chester were trout fishing in the mountain stream that ran through Buford's property. Actually, Chester was chasing anything that rustled in the bushes, so the fishing was up to Buford.

During one of Chester's skirmishes in the thick underbrush of the trees beside the stream, Buford heard a mind-numbing, heart-stopping shriek from Chester and then sudden quiet. Buford threw down his fishing pole and dashed into the underbrush just in time to see a brown bear lumbering away from the scene of his crime. Chester lay motionless on the ground, bleeding from a deep gash in his neck.

A short time later, Dad just happened to stop by Buford's house on his way to help another farmer patch his barn roof. He saw Buford carefully making his way to the house carrying the bleeding and seemingly lifeless Chester. Gently laying Chester on a blanket snatched from the porch, Buford looked pleadingly into my father's face and said, "Parson, please pray."

Without hesitation Dad gingerly placed his hand on Chester's gaping wound and prayed. That prayer was followed by several visits from the neighboring vet. Amazingly, Chester began to rally. Within a few months, Buford and Chester were fishing again. Chester sat on the bank right next to Buford and never ventured into the underbrush again.

One day as Dad and Buford shared a cup of way-too-strong coffee, Buford told Dad the vet had not expected Chester to live, his wound was so deep. Buford told the vet the reason Chester lived was because God cottoned to him. Then a slow smile spread across Buford's face, and he said, "Ya know, Parson, I think God cottons to me too."

Now, I hurry to point out that God doesn't have to perform a miracle in our lives or answer a specific prayer so that we can be assured He likes us. In fact, miracles rarely happen, and the prayers we whisper in direst need aren't always answered the way we want. Many of us are living out stories that have a completely different ending from that of Buford and Chester's story. We've experienced the heartache of losing someone we've cherished, a beloved daughter or son or other loved one, or even a dog. The important thing for us as we live out these stories with the not-so-happy endings is to get past faulty thinking and shaky faith to remember that God's love for us endures forever.

Occasionally we're blessed, as Buford was, to have someone like my dad come alongside to walk us through the heartache and remind us that God's Word promises He cottons to us, no matter what. We know the promise is true. And yet, sometimes, especially when we're alone, with our backs against the wall, it simply seems too hard to live out this kind of faith. That's the category of faulty thinking we'll examine next.

1. You know Scripture says you are loved, but do you truly believe that? Why or why not?

2. What events in your life cause you to question God's love for you? Do you recognize any faulty thinking?

3. How do you react to the last-minute conversion of the thief on the cross? Was it too simple? What does that say to those who work hard to please God?

Faith is hard

Passengers on a small commuter plane are waiting for the flight to leave. They're getting a little impatient, but the flight attendant assures them the pilots will be there soon and the plane will take off. Eventually two men dressed in pilot uniforms feel their way down the jet bridge and through the plane's door. Both are wearing dark glasses; one is using a guide dog, and the other is tapping his way along the aisle with a cane.

Nervous laughter spreads through the cabin as the men enter the cockpit, the door closes behind them, and the engines start up. The passengers begin glancing nervously around, searching for some sign that this is just a little practical joke. None is forthcoming. The plane zooms faster and faster down the runway, and the people sitting in the window seats realize they're headed straight for the water at the edge of the airport territory.

As it begins to look as though the plane will plow into the water, panicked screams fill the cabin. At that moment, the plane lifts smoothly into the air. The passengers relax and laugh a little sheepishly, and soon all retreat into their magazines, secure in the knowledge that the plane is in good hands.

In the cockpit, the copilot turns to the pilot and says, "You know, Bob, one of these days they're gonna scream too late, and we're all gonna die."

Would it be too great a stretch to say this story illustrates the complicated way many of us look at faith, especially when we think we're supposed to have (pun definitely intended) *blind* faith?

Now bear with me here. The blind pilots depended upon the sighted passengers to scream at the right time so the pilots would know when to manipulate whatever lifted the plane off the ground just before it would otherwise hit the water. I'd call that a pretty hard thing to do. The passengers, prior to screaming, settled into their seats, having faith that somehow the pilots knew what they were doing and could see where they were going. I'd call that blind faith, and it seems just as difficult.

But the truth is, faith is neither hard nor blind. But a lot of us insist on clinging to the faulty thinking that it is.

Falling for Faulty Thinking

I worked as a camp counselor one summer after my freshman year of college. The job, which included cohabiting with bugs, sleeping outdoors in a sleeping bag, and partaking of navy beans as the primary food offering, was not suited to my sensibilities. Most troubling of all was the game we taught new campers each week called the Trust Fall.

After teams were chosen, one team member (it could be a boy or a girl, but for our purposes we'll say it was a guy) would stand blindfolded with his back to his teammates and wait for the command, "Fall now!" The trusting one would then stiffen his body and slowly (depending on the gravity that day) fall backward into the locked hands and arms of his teammates. Their job was, of course, to prevent him from hitting the ground, thus avoiding bodily injury.

After the fall there would be a discussion about the level of trust each young camper exhibited. If the camper found it too hard to play the game—if he was reluctant to fall backward— it was assumed he had "trust issues." If he fell back with no hesitation, he was lauded as one who was secure about his "supporting environment." It was implied that his blind trust in those around him would one day qualify him for positions of great leadership.

I hated that game. It seemed to me it created an unfair hierarchy separating those who fell blindly from those who found it too hard to do. The easy fallers hung together with a tinge of superiority while the non-fallers ate their navy beans in isolation.

I finally took my complaint to the head counselor, Blue Jay. (We all had bird names. I was Swallow, which was an irony since I could barely get the food down.) I called Blue Jay "Woodpecker" in my mind but not to her face. She had a machine-gun-like way of speaking, and I suspected had probably been an "easy faller" in her day. She exuded more than just a tinge of superiority. When I told her my concern about the social hierarchy the Trust Fall game created, she dismissed me tersely with, "That's life, Miss Swallow. They might as well learn that fact now."

Fortunately, I developed a hearty pneumonia from repeated sleep-outs on the damp ground. Woodpecker reluctantly let me resign my position, but only when she got a note from my doctor verifying that, indeed, Miss Swallow was ill-suited to the rigors of camping and that her lungs were "alarmingly full of fluid."

The minute I was freed from "Bird Camp," my lungs released their alarming quantity of fluid. I got a job as a part-time nanny of a darling little five-year-old whom I sheltered from anything as daunting as the Trust Fall game, as well as from navy beans.

Many people seem inclined to consider faith a more or less blind system of belief while others just can't quite fall for it. It seems too hard to do, blindly believing without any evidence. The Danish philosopher Kierkegaard referred to the need for a "leap of faith" to enter into a realm of spirituality. The blind pilots took that leap, as did the passengers. My little campers were encouraged to do the same.

But thinking that faith is a hard, complicated concept that must be blindly accepted is faulty thinking, because viewing faith as "blind" totally misses the scriptural teaching of what faith is. When the Bible describes blindness, it is an image representing people who have chosen sin as a way of living. They walk in darkness. The plan of God is to call people out of the darkness. Blindness (a darkened soul slathered in sin) has one cure: Jesus. When we have faith in Him, we come out of darkness and into the light. Isaiah 42:16 (KJV) states this truth: "I will bring the blind by a way that they knew not; I will lead them in paths that they have not known: I will make darkness light before them, and crooked things straight. These things will I do."

> *Faith cannot be blind, because faith is*
> *authored by He who leads us to the light.*

Eyewitness, Jaw-Dropping Evidence

Faith cannot be blind, because faith is authored by He who leads us to the light.

The word *faith* means "trust." To trust God is not an act of blind, unreasonable belief, because God proves Himself to be utterly trustworthy at all times. There are many reasons to trust Him; several of them are in the apostle Peter's New Testament writings, in which he recounts his first-person experiences with Jesus.

Peter was a new man in his trust in Jesus after Jesus died and rose again. Peter talked to Him, ate with Him, was encouraged by Him, and then witnessed Jesus's ascending into heaven from the earth. These were facts Peter witnessed. He trusted those facts. They were not a part of some unreasonable belief system based upon fable or superstition. They were the truth, and Peter was passionate about that truth. He wrote in 2 Peter 1:16–18,

> We were not making up clever stories when we told you about the power of our Lord Jesus Christ and his coming again. We have seen his majestic splendor with our own eyes. And he received honor and glory from God the Father when God's glorious, majestic voice called down from heaven, "This is my beloved Son; I am fully pleased with him." We ourselves heard the voice when we were there with him on the holy mountain.

Peter was determined that the people to whom he spoke about Jesus knew He truly did come to earth as had been planned centuries before Bethlehem. Peter went on to say, in verses 19–21, that because he and the others heard the voice of God and saw His Son, "we have even greater confidence in the message proclaimed by the prophets. Pay close attention to what they wrote, for their words are like a light shining in a dark place—until the day Christ appears and his brilliant light shines in your hearts."

Peter then underscored his reasons for faith by reminding his listeners and readers that "no prophecy in Scripture ever came from the prophets themselves or because they wanted to prophesy. It was the Holy Spirit who moved the prophets to speak from God" (vv. 20–21).

There you have it. Christianity is not based on myths or other made-up stories. It is based on the testimony of those who witnessed jaw-dropping evidence that God sent His Son, Jesus, to this earth. These are not stories of blind faith. They are facts we can trust, facts that inspire faith.

We have other facts that inspire faith as well. We trust, or have faith, that God exists. Though we can't literally see God, we do see Him in what He has created, and that creation is visible to all persons. Romans 1:20 says, "From the time the world was created, people have seen the earth and sky and all that God made. They can clearly see his invisible qualities—his eternal power and divine nature. So they have no excuse whatsoever for not knowing God."

A Track Record of Trustworthiness

Let's go back now to the familiar faith definition found in Hebrews 11:1–2: "What is faith? It is the confident assurance that what we hope for is going to happen. It is the evidence of things we cannot see."

The fact that we cannot see the evidence does not make our faith blind. Our faith is not in that which is observable. It is placed on God. He is the One who knows what will happen in the future.

Second Corinthians 5:7 says, "We live by believing and not by seeing." Believing in whom? God. Not seeing what? The next step. The future. We believe Him to be trustworthy with the future . . . with whatever "is going to happen." We trust Him with the future because He has a track record of trustworthiness in the past. We look back on our lives and recognize the sovereign orchestration of the events of our lives and say, "That was God's doing!"

Psalm 77:11–12 states, "I recall all you have done, O Lord; I remember your wonderful deeds of long ago. They are constantly in my thoughts. I cannot stop thinking about them."

God told Abraham he would father generations of people whose numbers would be greater than the stars one could see in the sky. Abraham believed God, even though if he looked at the evidence, he would see a wife beyond childbearing years, and he would probably question his own potency. Today you and I see the fulfillment of God's promise to Abraham: the Jewish people from Isaac's line and the Arab people from Ishmael's line. That's a pack of people! Abraham did not live long enough to see God's promise totally fulfilled. But *we* see it, and our faith is nourished as a result of seeing the evidence of God's fulfilled promise to Abraham. We think back on those past remembrances of God's promises to His people, and that makes us want to think back on our own remembrances of God's promises to us.

He gave me more than I asked for.
I wanted earth stuff; He gave me heaven stuff.

The key to understanding the phrase "assurance that what we hope for is going to happen" is remembering that God has an eternal perspective and we do not. God is not a kindly old grandfather in the sky mindlessly doling out the treats His kids keep asking for. His plan for us is that we come to a deeper understanding of His purpose for us. That understanding is not measured in treats. In fact, that understanding may include experiencing the death of a baby or a husband or suffering some other tragedy that drives us to our wits' end and slams our backs against the wall. These are not "treat experiences," but they are maturity-building experiences. The times I have felt closest to God have been when my requested treats have been withheld. He gave me more than I asked for. I wanted earth stuff; He gave me heaven stuff.

So let's ask the questions again: Is faith blind? Is it hard to have faith?

Absolutely, faith is not blind. And it's not a mindless leap into the unknown that's too hard for us to fathom. Faith enables reason to go beyond its human limitations. But faith is not a simple result of reason; it is reason submitting to the truth of Scripture, which is saturated with and enlivened by the Holy Spirit of God. There are mysteries of faith that lie beyond my human understanding, but I believe them because they are rooted in the strength of God's Word. I don't pretend to understand the mystery of His ways, but Scripture describes God in ways that satisfy my mind. Scripture uses the testimony of eyewitnesses, and that also satisfies my mind.

Reason is a gift of God. It is, in fact, a part of the God-imprint we all carry. God encourages us to use the gift of reason. He challenged Israel to come and reason with Him in Isaiah 1:18: "'Come now, let us argue this out,' says the LORD." In the New Testament we see the apostles' eagerness to reason with their audiences about the credentials of the gospel. The book of Romans is one sustained argument by Paul, whose powers of rationality and extensive training were used by the Spirit of God for God's purpose of drawing His creation into an acceptance of who He was, is, and will always be.

Faith is not blind. Faith speaks to that God-placed center within us all that recognizes truth. We choose to believe that truth. We choose to embrace that truth. And we choose to live by faith, which is trustworthy.

I am not advocating an academic or sterile approach to our faith, but I am thrilled that it can stand up to scrutiny. Faith produces in us responses that go far beyond our scrutiny once our scrutiny is satisfied. In his book *How Now Shall We Live?* Chuck Colson said it well: "Christian faith is not an irrational leap. Examined objectively, the claims of the Bible are rational propositions well supported by reason and evidence."

Choosing to Believe

If faith does not require the too-hard action of trust falling or blind leaping, what *does* it require? It requires choosing: choosing to believe. For example, I choose to believe the evidence I see of God in His creation. I can't deny that creative power came from somewhere. I choose to believe it came from God and occurred exactly as described to us in Scripture. Genesis 1:2–3 tells us, "The earth was empty, a formless mass cloaked in darkness. And the Spirit of God was hovering over its surface. Then God said, 'Let there be light,' and there was light."

In addition to God the Father of all creation is Jesus, the Son, who "was with God, and he was God. He was in the beginning with God. He created everything there is. Nothing exists that he didn't make. Life itself was in him, and this life gives light to everyone. The light shines through the darkness, and the darkness can never extinguish it" (John 1:1–5).

I also choose to believe the Word of God, and when I am at my wits' end I crawl into its pages so my spirit can be enlivened, strengthened, and enabled to believe beyond what I see. The Bible is my faith object. It is crucial to my spiritual balance and my understanding of the degree to which God loves me. I choose to receive into my spirit the words of Psalm 31:7: "I am overcome with joy because of your unfailing love, for you have seen my troubles, and you care about the anguish of my soul."

Not only is my soul comforted by the words I read in Scripture, but I am also instructed by those words. I learn what faith is. Faith is not as complicated as I have sometimes made it. It is not hard. Quite simply, faith is a gift, and this gift is mine for the taking. It is not a gift I work to be worthy of or can work to achieve. As is true of any gift, I reach out for it. I accept it from the hand of God my Father. Ephesians 2:8 reminds me, "God saved you by his special favor when you believed. And you can't take credit for this; it is a gift from God." My part in all this is to accept the gift, to believe in the giver of the gift and then in the gift itself. I trust. I believe. I receive Jesus as Savior. Faith initiates that process.

If faith is not hard, why then does it *seem* hard? Why do

we feel at times that we are not walking in faith? Once again, may I suggest, our thinking may be faulty. Our thinking can lead us away from the gift and cause us to muddle about with misperceptions. One such misperception many Christians struggle with is the faulty thought that they don't have as much faith as other people do—that some have it, but they don't. Do you suppose these are the grownups who didn't do the Trust Fall when they were kids at camp? Are they continuing to eat their navy beans in isolation? In the next chapter we'll consider whether one's faith can be too small.

1. Do you think faith is hard? Why or why not?

2. What is the hardest element of faith for you?

3. Why do you have good reason to have faith in God? What evidence can you give that your faith is not blind?

4. Do you have any faulty thinking about faith? What is that faulty thinking and how can you change it?

Faulty Thought No. 5:

My faith is too small

When my husband, Ken, was diagnosed with pancreatic cancer, we marshaled all our faith troops together. Scores of people prayed for his healing; we anointed him with oil. In faith we claimed and believed he would experience regenerating life for every cell in his body.

He died fourteen months after his diagnosis.

Was our faith not big enough? Strong enough? Tenacious enough? Would he have lived if we'd found the right "faith person" to pray for him? When our faith failed to move mountains, could someone else's prayers and faith have saved Ken?

My mother's gift of faith and intercessory prayer often ripped the top off seemingly immovable mountains. I knew as a child that though Dad, as a pastor, was the public person, Mom was the faith person. Both my father and I would seek out the encouragement of her gentle but unwavering faith. Early in life my thought about faith was that some have it and some don't, and I believed I fell into the "don't have it" category. For that reason I wanted always to be near my mom's faith center. (That thinking may be one reason I felt such empathy for the kids who couldn't do the Trust Fall at camp.)

When Joani was born with spina bifida, I was certain she would be healed. The source of my certainty? My mother's powerful prayers of faith. But Joani died when she was fifteen days old. I might have more easily understood her death if I had been the only one praying. But my mother was praying; she was the "right faith person," but . . .

I received a letter last week from a brokenhearted mother whose seventeen-year-old son was heavily involved in the drug scene in their small rural community. Everyone knew everyone. Everyone knew her once-straight-A-student son was blowing his academic scholarship by suddenly failing all his classes.

I was surprised by her question to me. I expected her to ask my thoughts on what might cause this model boy to suddenly veer off onto such a destructive path. Instead, she said, "Faith has never been easy for me, and I know for sure I don't have enough to get my son straightened out. I need to find someone who has a lot of faith. Can you help me?"

Our Total, Complete, and Forever Source of Faith

I certainly understood her feelings of faith-barrenness and her feeling that someone somewhere has to do the faith thing for her. But do you recognize the faulty thinking not only in her but in me as well? Somehow I too felt I had to find a "faith person" for my husband and baby because I feared I wasn't sufficiently faith-endowed. There is nowhere in Scripture that says God has a faith camp where some of His children "have it" and some don't. That thinking is totally unscriptural and a whopper example of faulty thinking. But I'll have to admit this thinking still seeps into my soul from time to time and says, *You need to find someone to believe for you, Marilyn. . . . Your faith is shaky. It's too small.*

Once again, we go to Scripture, our faith object, and remind ourselves of a very basic truth. Hebrews 12:2 (NKJV) calls Jesus "the author and finisher of our faith." Our faith source is Jesus. He is the author of my faith. He is the giver of my faith. I am not. My mother was not. Any other person is not. Jesus gave me faith when I received Him into my heart and life. That faith is totally, personally my Jesus-given faith.

> *We all get in trouble with our faith lives*
> *when we forget we ourselves are not the author*
> *and finisher of our faith.*

The fear that our faith is too feeble for Christ to accept is illustrated in Mark 9:24. When Jesus encountered the boy with the demon, the father begged Jesus to heal the boy. Jesus told the father that anything is possible if a person believes. The father's poignant response was, "I do believe; help my unbelief" (NASB). The father seemed to recognize his source of faith was Jesus, but the father also recognized his faith was shaky . . . so he asked for help with it.

We all get in trouble with our faith lives when we forget we ourselves are not the authors and finishers of our faith. We do not earn our salvation; we do not earn our faith. Jesus is our total, complete, and forever source of faith. We must know Him, rely on Him, and accept the fact that all of our strength and competency comes from Him. To know that fact and trust in it is to have faith. That is the meaning of Paul's words in Philippians 4:13 (NIV): "I can do everything through him

[Jesus] who gives me strength." Jesus said, "Apart from me you can do nothing" (John 15:5).

Years ago I read an article by Horatius Bonar that gently clarified a few of my faith misperceptions. Bonar was a Scottish Presbyterian minister well known in the nineteenth century for his scholarly writings as well as for his writing of hymns and religious tracts. Though you may fear the hint of "dull" here, I promise you it is not. You will love the wisdom of his words.

Bonar encouraged believers to remember that apart from connecting us to Jesus, faith has no merit. Faith is the cable . . . the rod . . . the conduit. Faith is not our savior. It was not faith that loved us and died for us. It was not faith that took our sins upon the cross, died, and rose again. It was Jesus. Faith connects us to Jesus. Jesus was the perfect, sinless sacrifice. My faith, in and of itself, is not perfect. In fact, it is imperfect. All faith, no matter how poor or weak, serves as our contact to that which is always perfect and never weak.

At our most feeble moments, barely able to lift our voices, faith connects us to the One whose ear is ever inclined to the voices of His children.

So what's your point, Marilyn?

Here's the point: God required a sinless, perfect sacrifice. Nowhere do we read that God requires a sinless, perfect *faith*. I can't present a perfect anything. My faith and your faith may sometimes be utterly feeble and weak. But that condition will still connect us to Jesus. It is then that we too can cry out, "Lord, I do believe; help my unbelief."

Changing Our Thinking about Faith

What I love about these clarifying thoughts about faith is that we can quit thinking our prayers will not be valued or heard unless those prayers first rank a high number on the Richter scale of faith. At our most feeble moments, barely able to lift our voices, faith connects us to the One whose ear is ever inclined to the voices of His children.

Now let's apply these thoughts to the situation of the woman who wrote to me about her son who had dropped into the drug scene. She said, "Faith has never been easy for me." The reality is, her faith is carried to the heart of God by the Son of God, no matter how hard faith seems to her or how weak it appears. That's a fact. That may be new thinking, but she can change her thinking and choose to believe what God says in His Word about her faith.

More good news about her faith is that it can grow. She need not continue thinking she is feeble and weak in her faith. Jesus talked about the mustard plant, an annual plant with very small seeds. It grows to a considerable size in Palestine. Jesus's listeners were well acquainted with the mustard plant and its tiny seeds. When the apostles said to Jesus, as recorded in Luke 17:5–6, "We need more faith; tell us how to get it," Jesus responded, "Even if you had faith as small as a mustard seed, . . . you could say to this mulberry tree, 'May God uproot you and throw you into the sea,' and it would obey you!'"

With all due respect, I don't find that a very satisfying answer.

I would like it if Jesus spelled out how to get more faith in an easy formula that I could slip into my purse. When I am feeling feeble, I could pull out the list . . . mutter over it . . . find the problem . . . and then fix it. But the whole thing about our spiritual walk is that it is not defined by formulas, and it's not my job to fix it.

Jesus said, "Believe." Then He walked away. My job is to remember I can choose to believe because it was He who authored my faith—enabled my faith in the first place. "I believe, Lord; help my unbelief." In other words, "Help me grow." And just look what can happen if my faith is no bigger than a mustard seed!

Paul said in Romans 10:17 that faith comes from hearing the Word of God. I grow, you grow, this dear mother grows by studying the Word of God. The Bible is our faith object. Our faith grows as we study it. This section of Romans 10 (vv. 8–13) is translated in *The Message* Bible this way:

> It's the word of faith that welcomes God to go to work and set things right for us. This is the core of our preaching. Say the welcoming word to God—"Jesus is my Master"—embracing, body and soul, God's work of doing in us what he did in raising Jesus from the dead. That's it. You're not "doing" anything; you're simply calling out to God, trusting him to do it for you. That's salvation. With your whole being you embrace God setting things right, and then you say it, right out loud: "God has set everything right between him and me!"
>
> Scripture reassures us, "No one who trusts God like this— heart and soul—will ever regret it. . . . Everyone who calls, 'Help, God!' gets help."

What fantastic encouragement these words from Scripture provide. Forgive me, but I'm going to throw out a formula I see in this Romans passage:

- I say the words "Help, God."

- I trust Him to help me.

- I remember I'm not doing anything; I'm calling out to God and trusting Him to do it for me.

Does this sound too easy? Too passive? Too laid back in my hammock and munching Milk Duds while God works? It is not passive at all, in that God not only invites our participation as He builds our faith lives, He requires it. You try lying back in your hammock, and He'll tip you out of it. You are in a loving partnership, but He's in charge. I first say the words, then I trust Him with my growth, and He takes over. But He takes me with Him.

So what about the hurting mother? These were my suggestions to her:

- Begin changing your thinking from *I'm not good at faith* to *Jesus gave me faith when I received Him.*

- Begin thinking, *My words are always, always presented lovingly to the Father, who always, always hears them.*

- Your new thinking takes you to Jesus-inspired faith: *I believe, Lord; help me.*

- Study His Word every day.

- Talk to Him daily in prayer if only by saying His name: "Jesus, Jesus, Jesus." There is more power in that name than in any word in any language in the universe.

- Memorize Psalm 34:17 and say it out aloud over and over: "The LORD hears his people when they call to him for help. He rescues them from all their troubles."

I also told her, "The God of the universe knows your son. He sees your son, and He cares for your son. Trust God to do what God plans to do. It may not be in your timing or your way, but when it is God's way the promise is, 'We know that God causes everything to work together for the good of those who love God and are called according to his purpose for them'"(Romans 8:28).

I continue to learn and relearn, myself, what I have suggested to this dear mother. Probably the greatest challenge to me is remembering God does it . . . I don't. That phrase from *The Message* translation quoted earlier, "trusting him to do it for you," should be great news. It is, in fact, great news. But I often have trouble not fussing about things . . . His timing, His way, even His character (if He really cares, why doesn't He change some things?).

Coming to an understanding and then acceptance of God's sovereignty has revolutionized my faith.

My greatest growth in these areas has been to truly, at the core of my being, learn to rest in His sovereign control. Coming to an understanding and then acceptance of God's sovereignty has revolutionized my faith: how I think, how I believe, how I feel, and how I interpret the events of my life. The doctrine of sovereignty is, to me, the most peace-producing, faith-enhancing, and rest-inspiring belief about God that I have experienced. I can't wait to think about it with you in our next chapter.

The Importance of United Prayer

But before we conclude this chapter, I want to say how vital, even crucial, I believe it to be for us to band together with other believers in prayer. My concern that we not use other people as "faith stand-ins" does not diminish the importance of our coming to the Father in united prayer. We are His children. We unite our hearts as a faith family, bringing our heart cries to Him. Jesus modeled for us the role of group prayer support as He implored the disciples to help bear His burden and pray for Him as He entered the Garden of Gethsemane.

The early church met regularly to pray together and to experience the growth of each person's faith in the company of one another. For us to "bear one another's burdens" (Galatians 6:2 NASB) requires sharing, requesting prayer support, and allowing ourselves to be vulnerable in each other's presence. In these ways we build one another up and further the work of the church. We remember Scripture says, "Where two or three have gathered together in My name, I am there in their midst" (Matthew 18:20 NASB). There's power in corporate prayer.

Paul reminds us in Ephesians 6:18 (MSG), "Pray hard and long. Pray for your brothers and sisters. Keep your eyes open. Keep each other's spirits up so that no one falls behind or drops out." There is no doubt we need to pray together, and by the same token, there is no doubt that when we are alone, we need to believe God hears us as clearly as He hears the giants of the faith. Remember:

> The LORD is near to all who call upon Him,
> To all who call upon Him in truth.
> He will fulfill the desire of those who fear Him;
> He also will hear their cry and save them.
> (Psalm 145:18–19 NKJV)

1. Discuss some times when you felt your faith was so small you needed someone else to believe for you. What's the faulty thinking here?

2. Discuss the meaning of the words "Faith apart from connecting us to Jesus has no merit. . . . Faith is not our savior."

3. What does Jesus's illustration of the mustard seed say to you?

4. Do you judge yourself for your frail faith? What would Jesus say to you about your faith?

Faulty Thought No. 6:
I don't like the plan

A year after Joani died, we adopted a baby girl who came to live with us when she was nine days old. Her name is Elizabeth (my mother's name), but we call her Beth. She was a bouncy, happy, totally cooperative little person who cheerfully performed her baby functions on schedule and seemingly with great delight.

We didn't adopt a baby to replace our eternity-destined baby, but by the same token, my mothering instinct longed to fill my arms and heart with a baby girl; God ordained that little girl for us. She was born August 16, 1967. Of that ordained fact I have no doubt. How can I be so sure? I find the proof in Ephesians 1:11 (NKJV), which includes the phrase "being predestined according to the purpose of Him who works all things according to the counsel of His will."

That verse has been life-changing for me as I consider, "all things . . . His will." When little Beth was conceived, her teenage parents were not married. Though they wanted to marry and provide a home for their baby, both sets of parents insisted the mother fly to California, where she would have her baby in anonymity and, may I add, shame. She would then return home to Chicago. Beth's parents would go back to high school in the fall. No one would know; life would go on.

Ken, Marilyn, and little Jeff then enter the picture and eagerly receive Beth as the fourth member of our family. We explained to Jeff that although I did not give birth to Beth,

another mommy did, and that God had created Beth for us . . .
our family . . . to be his little sister.

All things . . . His will.

We thrived. When Beth was a junior at Westmont College
she became interested in investigating her biological roots. We
had told her the little we knew, and she'd seemed more than
satisfied with the circumstances of her birth. We always
couched it in theological terms: "God chose you to be in our
family." But as a psychology major, she wanted to fill in the
gaps and go beyond the theological. She wanted to understand
the feelings that accompanied the decision to "adopt her out."
She wanted to know what had happened to those teenage kids.
Did they wish they had kept her? Did they ever think about
her? Did they just go their separate ways after she was born?

All things . . . His will.

Shortly after Ken's death in 1990, Beth began the search for
her biological parents. She found them in Naperville, Illinois.
Sherry and Steve Booth had married, and Sherry had given
birth to three more children. Steve had gone on to college and
seminary. He is a Baptist minister. Yes, they wished they could
have kept Beth. Yes, they thought about her. In fact, they
prayed that maybe God would let them meet her, maybe even
get to know her someday.

All things . . . His will.

Within weeks after Beth's first meeting with Sherry, Steve,
and the other three siblings—Amy, Laura, and Eric—Steve
decided to tell his congregation about their "love child," the
child no one knew existed except for Steve, Sherry, and their
respective parents. The baby I thought was chosen for Ken,

Marilyn, and Jeff was going to be introduced to a group of church people along with Steve and Sherry's brothers and sisters as their "lost-and-found child."

> *If ever I experienced a sovereignly*
> *designed moment I hated, it was then.*

On that designated Sunday morning, I sat in Steve's church in Illinois with Jeff, his wife, Carla, and Beth, watching and listening as the congregation tried to fathom the story of their pastor's youthful indiscretion. He stood hand in hand with Sherry, acknowledging their sin, God's forgiveness, the call to the ministry, and now, the most tangible touch of grace they had ever known, the return of the baby they never wanted to give up: Beth. She was then invited to join Steve and Sherry at the front of the church. By the time Beth reached the platform, the congregation members had gathered their wits about them and were clapping thunderously. If ever I experienced a sovereignly designed moment, it was then.

If ever I experienced a sovereignly designed moment I hated, it was then.

All things . . . His will.

Feeling Argumentative about It All

I'll talk about my perfectly reasonable emotions later, but let's first discuss just what Scripture means by "all things . . . His will." Scripture, our faith object, teaches that it is God who is in control of everything on earth and in heaven:

- Psalm 115:3: "For our God is in the heavens, and he does as he wishes."

- Psalm 89:11: "The heavens are yours, and the earth is yours; everything in the world is yours—you created it all."

- Jeremiah 10:23: "I know, LORD, that a person's life is not his own. No one is able to plan his own course."

- Proverbs 19:21: "You can make many plans, but the LORD's purpose will prevail."

It is impossible to wiggle past this gigantic truth: God is in control of all things. He is sovereign. On a human level, one who is sovereign is a king or a queen, a ruler. He or she has all the power. On a divine level, God is our Ruler: He has all the power. No one reigns over Him. First Timothy 6:15 says God is "the blessed and only Ruler, the King of kings and Lord of lords" (NIV). In the Old Testament King David described God this way in 1 Chronicles 29:11–12:

> Yours, O LORD, is the greatness, the power, the glory, the victory, and the majesty. Everything in the heavens and on earth is yours, O LORD, and this is your kingdom. We adore you as the one who is over all things. Riches and honor come from you alone, for you rule over everything. Power and might are in your hand, and it is at your discretion that people are made great and given strength.

Our task is to give up our desire for control and relinquish our will into the sovereign hands of God. These convincing verses certainly make God's divine kingship clear, but many of us continue to fuss about the word *all,* even as we attempt to acknowledge God is sovereign and hand Him our wills. When God says He is in control of "all" things, we get a little argumentative and say, "Surely God does not mean absolutely everything. Surely there are a few things we're in control of." For example, we say, "God was not in control of Steve and Sherry's sin; they were on their own with that one . . . weren't they?"

> *Our task is to give up our desire for*
> *control and relinquish our wills into the*
> *sovereign hands of God.*

Of course God does not author sin. We are, indeed, on our own when we sin, but God is there to sovereignly orchestrate the aftermath of sin. In fact, sin is used to bring about His higher good for us as well as His preordained purpose.

One of God's "higher goods" for Sherry and Steve was that God's loving, forgiving, and grace-oriented nature be made abundantly clear to them. God's grace-oriented nature was made clear not only to Sherry and Steve but to all who witnessed it. Steve's church members have the good fortune of seeing a living, walking example of how God forgives sin and then blesses the sinner— which is, incidentally, every single person in the congregation.

I have written this story before in other books. Those who have read the story are encouraged to believe that even if they've sinned, God will not walk away from them, saying, "I can never use you in public ministry. Your sin was too great. I forgive your sin, but your future usefulness is limited." God's higher purposes will not be thwarted. Why? Because He is in control of all things.

Recognizing God's Higher Purposes

My understanding as well as my appreciation of God's sovereignty—"All things . . . His will"—have grown enormously as a result of this experience. To begin with, neither of my children belongs to me; they belong to the God who created them. Though Jeff's human origins began with my biological union with Ken, I have absolutely no claim to Jeff. I love him fiercely, but he is not mine. I am responsible *to* both my children, but I am no longer responsible *for* them. They are responsible for themselves. They are responsible to God for their relationship with Him; I am not. I am grateful they both love Jesus and seek to fulfill His purposes for their lives, but I've let them go. I've entrusted them to God's sovereign care. I pray for them daily, love them deeply, and beat a path to their doors as often as possible. They are great kids . . . even if they aren't mine!

Now, as long as we're on the subject, let me say this. I have encouraged both Jeff and Beth to not feel responsible for me either. They are, and will always be, responsible *to* me. That means they are a loving, thoughtful, sensitive presence to me as I hope always to be to them. But neither child is responsible for my emotions. My emotions are my responsibility, not theirs.

So when Beth asked if I would be OK with the resumption of her parent-search so soon after Ken died, I told her to go ahead. She'd started the search before Ken's diagnosis, but when we got that sobering news, she, as we all did, put everything on hold. We chose to walk every step of the cancer path with Ken. When he went on to a cancer-free eternity, we picked up the strands of our lives and began the process of moving on. I encouraged Beth in her search.

> *The last thing I want for either of my children*
> *is for them to feel the decisions of their lives must first*
> *be OK with Mom's emotions.*

Did I feel good about it? No! But that response was mine to deal with. I told her how I felt but that I also trusted God's sovereign timing. I knew she was to continue the path she was on. God had placed her on that path.

The last thing I want for either of my children is for them to feel the decisions of their lives must first be OK with Mom's emotions. I am pleased that I seem never to be out of the loop of anything they are doing. They seek my counsel, hear my responses, and also know I will support their decisions apart from my emotions. I'm convinced that any parent who refuses to let go of his or her children or makes them feel guilty when they seek independence is going to be a deeply resented parent.

Now, of course I have also told them there will come a day when they will have to assume responsibility *for* me as well as *to* me. When I start doing rude and crude things in public or kissing strangers in the park, the time has come! Until then, the leash is long, but the bond is strong.

Now, back to the subject of who belongs to whom. Beth does not belong to Sherry and Steve. They waited twenty-three years to meet her and are even now continuing to know her, but she belongs to God. So when I sat in Steve's church years ago and thought, *Beth was chosen for Ken, Marilyn, and Jeff*, I was engaging in some faulty thinking. She was chosen for a purpose higher than membership in a specific family. She is the recipient of much human love from both families, but for me, she has served as a reminder to let go of what was never mine.

All things . . . His will.

Just because we know, believe, and have faith in God's sovereign design does not mean we like the design. We may actually hate the design. I felt that way as I sat in Steve's church and watched "that family" hugging and crying on the platform; I felt Jeff's resistance as he sat next to me. There was another brother up there; that was not easy for Jeff. It still is not. And I'll have to admit to a small pew-pity-party as I sat there. Jeff had just gotten married. Beth had "that family" up there on the platform, and I, in my newly widowed state, would board a plane alone later that day and eventually walk into an empty house back in California, muttering, "Not crazy about Your plan, God."

Did I dare tell God I was not crazy about His plan? Of course. He already knew my feelings. He knew what my feelings would be long before I had the experience that produced those feelings. He knows the beginning from the end, including my emotions. So I told Him what He already knew. And He received my emotions.

How do I know? My faith object tells me He knows that humans "are as frail as breath" (Isaiah 2:22). It also tells me, "All humanity finds shelter in the shadow of your wings" (Psalm 36:7).

I felt my frailty; I experienced His shelter. That does not mean I liked the plan, but I was quieted in my soul as I realized the part designed for me by the God who knew a baby girl would be born to teenage parents on August 16, 1967. He knew that baby would be lovingly raised by people He sovereignly selected, who would not be her biological parents. He knew she would meet her biological parents and develop a relationship with them and that it would be healing for all of them. He also knew that reunion would hurt me. He was not indifferent to my hurt but drew me gently ever and ever closer to His huge truth: "'I know the plans I have for you,' says the LORD. 'They are plans for good and not for disaster, to give you a future and a hope'" (Jeremiah 29:11).

A part of experiencing His shelter, referenced in Psalm 36:7, is trusting the One who provides that shelter. In the passage from Jeremiah, He promises me His plans are meant to give me "a future and a hope." I settle into the comfort of that sheltering promise, even though I may not yet feel the hope He promised. But I trust Him and have faith in His character of love that a higher good is in the making and that one day, I will look back and say, "Ah, yes . . . God's hand was in that."

If God is indeed the sovereign Ruler over all things and all things are predestined according to His purpose, what does that mean then to me as a mother whose child was born with spina bifida? Was that a preordained experience for Ken, Marilyn, and little Jeff? Surely this is one of those times when we can legitimately say, "Well . . . maybe not *all* things. Just most things."

Were those my thoughts, I'd be guilty of faulty thinking. God is not just a *trifle* sovereign; He does not have just a *touch* of sovereignty. He is totally sovereign. That means we have to drag back the word *all* and think it . . . believe it . . . trust it . . . and have faith in the One who enables our faith.

We'll consider these thoughts again in the next chapter, but I want to leave you with another "all things" verse:

We know that all things work together for good to those who love God, to those who are the called according to His purpose. (Romans 8:28 NKJV)

That *all* is my key to understanding God's heart toward me . . . His heart toward you and toward all of us as we seek His sovereign shelter when we're feeling frail, with our backs against the wall.

1. Do you believe God is in control of "all" things? Do you draw a line somewhere and say there are a few things He is not in control of? If so, where do you draw the line?

2. Since God does not ordain sin, how can we say He is in control of all things?

3. Discuss some times in your life when it did not appear to you God was in control.

Faulty Thought No. 7:
I might drown

With floodwaters rising rapidly from the neighborhood's rain-engorged creek, two women, Wilda and Mona, scrambled to the rooftops of their respective homes. They began to chat back and forth about the height of the water and speculated about how long they'd be perched on their roofs.

In the midst of these concerns, Wilda noticed a blue baseball cap moving steadily on top of the water: first to the left then switching directions and moving steadily to the right. Nothing was visible beneath the cap, only its back-and-forth movement. Fascinated, Wilda called Mona over to notice the blue baseball cap. Mona responded with, "Oh, that's Basil. He said he was going to mow the yard today come hell or high water."

I have a touch of Basil in me. Sometimes I'm so determined to slosh through my daily duties, I don't realize I'm on the verge of drowning in the process. One of those sloshing, near-drowning times for me was the months following Joani's death.

I had not yet done a full study on what the sovereignty of God meant and certainly had no thought of applying it to that loss. It was then just one of those doctrines I didn't quite get, and the part I got I didn't like. So I stayed away from it. What jolted me back into thinking about it was a balmy California evening Ken and I spent with Chuck and Cynthia Swindoll.

They had only recently assumed the pastorate of the church

Ken and I attended. We all felt an instant click of kinship for one another and got together as often as possible. On that pivotal evening, Chuck asked Ken and me about Joani. Among other things, Chuck wanted to know where we placed God in that experience.

I was surprised by his question because the answer seemed so obvious for believers. But I leaped in ahead of Ken and said something to the effect that we live in an imperfect world where sin runs rampant and that sin-run world includes malformations in babies.

I expected to be praised for my sensible grasp of theological truth when Chuck asked simply, "What was God's part in her life?"

"Well," I said, slightly irritated, "He took her to heaven when she died."

"He did much more than that," Chuck said softly. "She was God's gift to you, ordained for His purposes for your life, for Ken's life, and for Jeff's."

I was twenty-six years old and knew I had a lot to learn about life, God, and other things, but I was momentarily silenced by Chuck's comment. In fact, I wasn't sure what he meant. We certainly looked on Joani's little being as a gift of God—all life was a gift of God—and though we were heartbroken, we experienced God's comfort and love. Was there more to it than that? What did Chuck mean by "ordained for His purposes"? Just exactly what *were* His purposes?

More troubling still was the question: Does God's ordaining include physical imperfections? Death? Pain? Those thoughts bothered my preconceived ideas about God. I knew

His Word promises to bring beauty from ashes, but does He have a hand in the ashes? Does He *ordain* ashes? That sounded like heresy to me. How dare I even think it?

This was very deep water for me. Ken backed off. It was more than just deep water for him.

Seeking Wisdom in the Unsearchable Mind of God

Thus my journey began. I in no way felt capable of figuring out what no one on earth has yet to figure out, namely, unraveling the mystery of God's mind. Our faith object makes clear that Marilyn will never, ever get into the mind of God and be able to say, "Ah, so *that's* what He's doing and *that's* why He's doing it." Instead, Scripture tells us,

> *Oh, the depth of the riches both of the wisdom and*
> *knowledge of God! How unsearchable are His judgments*
> *and His ways past finding out!*
>
> *"For who has known the mind of the LORD?*
> *Or who has become His counselor?"*
> *(Romans 11:33–34 NKJV)*

The irony here is that I'm told God's ways are "past finding out," and yet I am encouraged to find out all I can within the parameters of His divine mystery. For example, Deuteronomy 4:29 (NKJV) says, "You will seek the LORD your God, and you will find Him if you seek Him with all your heart and with all your soul." Now, of course that verse does not promise I'm going to understand it all, but it does encourage me to seek Him out.

I'm told God's ways are "past finding out,"
and yet I am encouraged to find out all I can within
the parameters of His divine mystery.

I began my search of more clearly understanding God's sovereign intent for my life by remembering that this world belongs to the enemy; Satan has been given certain rights to this earth for a period of time. Jesus referred to him as the "ruler of this world," but Jesus also said that ruler would one day be "cast out" (John 12:31 NKJV). He has limited time here as the world's ruler, but even so, I have to know how to deal with him as well as recognize his tactics. Otherwise I might blame God for what Satan authors.

For example, God does not author sin. He also never tempts us to sin. If we yield to temptation, Satan has a victory party. God will not abandon us to the aftermath of sin. When we seek His forgiveness, a higher purpose will always be ours because our sin never leaves God in a paralysis; nothing is wasted in His economy. But Satan wants to wear us down with arguments that distract from grace and forgiveness. It is not God's sovereign will that we sin . . . ever. But it is *always* Satan's intent.

An illuminating picture of God's sovereignty is seen in the book of Job. The picture is of Satan having to get permission to "test" one of God's creations, Job. Even though Satan is the ruler of this world, divine restrictions were put upon him. He did not have any power over Job beyond what God granted. I find this a fascinating conversation, especially this opening round of negotiations:

> One day the angels came to present themselves before the LORD, and Satan the Accuser came with them. "Where have you come from?" the LORD asked Satan. And Satan answered the LORD, "I have been going back and forth across the earth, watching everything that's going on."
>
> Then the LORD asked Satan, "Have you noticed my servant Job? He is the finest man in all the earth—a man of complete integrity. He fears God and will have nothing to do with evil."
>
> Satan replied to the LORD, "Yes, Job fears God, but not without good reason! You have always protected him and his home and his property from harm. You have made him prosperous in everything he does. Look how rich he is! But take away everything he has, and he will surely curse you to your face!"
>
> "All right, you may test him," the LORD said to Satan. "Do whatever you want with everything he possesses, but don't harm him physically." (Job 1:6–12)

(Later, God did give Satan permission to harm Job physically.)

There are a few major understandings I got out of that conversation that help me:

1. Satan was doing what he is doing even today. He was "going back and forth across the earth, watching everything that's going on." The earth is his; he eyeballs it constantly. What's he looking for? First Peter 5:8 (NKJV) answers the question: "Be

sober, be vigilant; because your adversary the devil walks about like a roaring lion, seeking whom he may devour."

2. Though the world belongs to Satan, all the power belongs to God. Satan cannot touch us unless God gives permission. Satan is on restriction. Were he not, the world scene would be even worse.

3. Satan used a surefire technique against Job. He took away everything Job valued: his homes, his money, his children, and his health, and then he watched to see how Job's faith held up under the weight of those losses. Satan is still using that technique. It works. I think Satan is the originator of "If it ain't broke, don't fix it." It's worked for centuries.

4. As Job reeled from all his losses, he began to anguish over what he had done to bring them on. Was it sin? Was it God's indifference to him? This part of the story illustrates another centuries-old technique used by Satan: make 'em scared and insecure, and convince 'em God does not care. "If He cared," goes Satan's logic, "all this would not have happened to you."

5. The most dangerous technique Satan uses is to get us to renounce God. "Walk away from Him just as He walked away from you," goes the enemy's logic. Job, though he complained mightily, would not renounce God even at the greatest extremity of his experience. Job's famous words were, "Though he slay me, yet will I trust Him" (Job 13:15 NKJV). Satan hated those words . . . hated that response. Satan failed his Job project.

[Satan's] goal is that we will walk away from God in despair and then disbelieve. God's goal is that we will stand up under testing and grow stronger in our faith and even more convinced of the Almighty's love.

There is another sovereign truth we learn in the Job account. It has to do with testing. God gave Satan permission to test Job. Satan is still in the testing business with each of us. His goal is that we will walk away from God in despair and then disbelieve. God's goal is that we will stand up under testing and grow stronger in our faith and even more convinced of the Almighty's love. First Peter 1:7 speaks of God's goal for our testing:

> These trials are only to test your faith, to show that it is strong and pure. It is being tested as fire tests and purifies gold—and your faith is far more precious to God than mere gold. So if your faith remains strong after being tried by fiery trials, it will bring you much praise and glory and honor on the day when Jesus Christ is revealed to the whole world.

So, does God sovereignly ordain our "fiery trials," or is that just Satan doing what he does? God gives permission. God wills us life in our trials; Satan wills us death from our trials. But in it all, God is still in control. And what about us? We have a choice. We can follow Job's example and refuse to renounce God, or we can tell God, "This is too much. My faith in You is destroyed. I had faith, but now I can't do it. How could You expect me to bear up under all this?"

God's Sovereign Ways

Let's take our discussion of sovereignty a step further. When we say that God is sovereign, we are saying He is in control of all things. Chuck Swindoll, in his book *The Mystery of God's Will*, says this:

> Sovereignty means our all-wise, all-knowing God reigns in realms beyond our comprehension to bring about a plan beyond our ability to alter, hinder, or stop. His plan includes all promotions and emotions. His plan can mean both adversity and prosperity, tragedy and calamity, ecstasy and joy. It envelops illness as much as health, perilous times as much as comfort, safety, prosperity, and ease. His plan is at work when we cannot imagine why, because it is so unpleasant, as much as when the reason is clear and pleasant. His sovereignty, though it is inscrutable, has dominion over all handicaps, all heartaches, all helpless moments. It is at work through all disappointments, broken dreams, and lingering difficulties. And even when we cannot fully fathom why, He knows. Even when we cannot explain the reasons, He understands. And when we cannot see the end, He is there, nodding, "Yes, that is my plan."

Lamentations 3:38 (NIV) reads, "Is it not from the mouth of the Most High that both calamities and good things come?" And Solomon wrote in Proverbs 21:1 (NASB), "The king's heart is like channels of water in the hand of the LORD; He turns it wherever He wishes." We are talking about a God who is in control, and not only is He in control, He orchestrates the events in life according to His own purpose. And that may include calamities.

Joni Eareckson Tada, best-selling author and riveting

speaker, broke her neck in a diving accident nearly forty years ago. As a quadriplegic she lives her life in a wheelchair, but she accomplishes more than any human being I know. In addition to writing and speaking, she sings and paints and is the founder and president of Joni and Friends, which, among many other services, provides wheelchairs and encouragement to millions of people around the world. I am in awe of her "in-spite-of" accomplishments.

More than anything Joni does, I am in awe of her sweet, non-blaming love for Jesus. I've wondered many times in the years I've known her, *How does she manage to stay upbeat in a world of too many downbeats?*

During a quick phone call last week, she told me she had broken her leg. Her specially equipped van came to a sudden stop, and Joni was thrown out of her restraining strap; the result, a broken leg.

My response as she told me this was, "Good grief, God! Hasn't she had enough? You didn't need to let that happen!"

Joni barely heard my blustering. She was more concerned with the study she is doing on the ethics of stem-cell research. She asked me to pray about several national television shows lined up to discuss her views on the subject.

Envisioning her with one broken, paralyzed leg propped up on a pillow, I tried to enter the larger picture of God's hand on Joni's life and pray accordingly. Once again I wondered how she manages to stay upbeat in a downbeat world. Of course I know the answer. She has chosen to have faith in the God whose sovereign ways she may not comprehend but whose character of love and compassion she trusts.

For years it seemed blasphemous to ever think God figured into the calamities of life. My assumption was that calamities originated with Satan's efforts to overthrow my soul's peace, joy, and equilibrium. And of course that is Satan's resolve, but God fits in there in ways I had refused to think about.

The God I know and love came to earth to heal and restore. He was compassionate and wept over death, and He ultimately conquered it by dying on the cross. How could anyone possibly assume God would choose suffering for us? How could He in love just stand by and let Joni break her neck? Or let my baby be victim to spina bifida or Ken to cancer? The list goes on for all of us.

The truth I've come to embrace is that God is indeed compassionate, loving, and kind. And yet I need to recognize another dimension of God; He is almost militantly in charge of all things. Deuteronomy 32:39 (NKJV) says,

> *Now see that I, even I, am He,*
> *And there is no God besides Me;*
> *I kill and I make alive;*
> *I wound and I heal;*
> *Nor is there any who can deliver from My hand.*

Those words are startling to those of us who would "fashion our God" into an image more to our liking. And yet I find enormous comfort in this no-nonsense strength of God. No one can "deliver from [His] hand." God is the initiator of all things. He is not Satan's errand boy tidying up messes Satan initiates. That would make God a reactor to an inferior power.

All things first go through the hand of God. He is the initiator. There is no greater power. Daniel 4:35 (NKJV) reads,

> *He does according to His will in the army of heaven*
> *And among the inhabitants of the earth.*
> *No one can restrain His hand*
> *Or say to Him, "What have You done?"*

The belief in God's sovereignty frees me to accept everything I have ever or will ever experience. Knowing all things are according to His will means I don't second-guess anything. I simply say, "Lord, let me rest in this experience even though I may not want it, like it, or understand it. You know what You intend to accomplish; You have the big picture, and I don't. Thank You that I don't have to spin my wheels trying to figure out, *Where did this come from and why?* It came from You in one way or another, and I choose to trust You in it."

Were I to have known this comforting assurance of God's sovereign design forty years ago, I'd have saved myself from much of the emotional deep water resulting from Joani's death. Today I humbly accept that God's ways are "past finding out" and that no one has "known the mind of the LORD" or "become His counselor." I will never know the heavenly pre-plan that accompanied her birth, but I do know the purpose of Joani's life was not to break my heart. It was to enlarge my heart. It was to expand my interior world, making room for deeper faith to grow and to allow respect for God's mystery to take root. As David prayed in Psalm 69:15 (NKJV), "Let not the floodwater overflow me, nor let the deep swallow me up."

It did not overflow me. That too was God's sovereign design.

All things . . . His will.

1. What does the sentence "God is sovereign" mean to you?

2. Discuss a time in your life when you found great comfort in God's sovereignty.

3. Does God's sovereignty ordain our "fiery trials" described in 1 Peter 1:7? Talk about one of your fiery trials. Where do you place God's sovereignty in that trial?

There's too much pain

I walked into a crowded room, and there he was. He grinned at me; I grinned back. His luminous brown eyes sparkled with fun and vivacity; they held me, refusing to look away. Yielding to that sweet force, I fell in love!

He who captured my heart was a six-year-old little boy from the province of Kwa-Zulu-Natal in South Africa. I was there with some of my fellow Women of Faith speakers and World Vision. The purpose of the trip was to document and hopefully minister to this population that has the highest AIDS infection rate in all of South Africa. This little boy's father had died of AIDS, and his mother is HIV-positive. And yet he was sitting happily in a hot classroom crowded with other children waiting for the visitors from America to drive up in their dusty van from Bergville.

As the World Vision cameraman panned across those little faces singing or reciting their lessons (all in the Zulu language) or simply watching us sing and recite our lessons (all in the English language), there was an infectious optimism in the room. My little heartthrob never took his eyes off me. The minute we finished filming, I motioned for him to come over to me, and within seconds he was in my lap. I hugged him tightly and told him I loved him. He hugged me back and reached for my dark glasses. In a flash they were on his face. He was giddy with triumph.

I had forgotten to change glasses when we left our van. My

dark glasses are a trifle gaudy: a combination of blue and purple swirls with metallic rims. My little heartthrob had fallen in love with my glasses and couldn't wait to get them off my face and onto his. My matronly self offered limited intrigue, but, oh, those eyeglass frames!

As if I hadn't given enough, he wanted the silver spoon ring I was wearing too. My dad had made the ring from my grandmother's sterling silver collection. As the little charmer slid the too-big ring onto his tiny finger, I clutched and selfishly thought, *I wonder if I'll get my stuff back.*

But he was not finished with me. He looked curiously into my mouth and motioned that he wanted to see the gum I was chewing. I pushed it forward between my teeth. With one quick swipe the gum was out of my mouth and into his. He settled back then into my lap, sporting my gaudy shades and my grandmother's silver spoon and chewing my Juicy Fruit gum. I was still in love.

As we concluded our visit with these darling little children, my heartthrob soberly handed me back my glasses and my ring. He made a motion to return the gum; I motioned for him to keep it. He watched until we were out of sight. I still have a lump in my throat as I remember the tears slowly rolling down his cheeks. My cheeks were wet too.

My heart hurts as I consider what an uncertain future he has. He's just a little boy living in an environment ravaged by AIDS. He will pay the price for choices he never made, but the consequences will be just as annihilating.

Max Lucado refers to the AIDS epidemic in Africa as the worst global disaster since the days of Noah. One wonders about God in such a disaster. He could scoop up these millions of victims and rescue them from the destructive path they have walked with such ignorance. God could cradle my little heart-throb and prevent all future hurt from coming to him.

We read accounts of the Holocaust, the Killing Fields of Cambodia, and the torture chambers in the Middle East. We see television coverage of hurricanes, floods, and earthquakes where thousands lose their lives, and we wonder about God.

I watch my good friend Barbara Johnson struggle with the effects of a brain tumor and think, *Not Barbara! She has given encouragement and hope to millions who read her books and hear her speak. Why should she end her years of fruitful ministry with a brain tumor? She has already suffered enormous human loss. This is not fair.*

What Kind of God Would Allow This?

A woman wrote to me last week and said she had always considered herself a woman of faith. She had raised her kids in the church and seen them all marry Christian spouses. But her faith in God's love, goodness, and protection was shattered when her son-in-law shot and killed her daughter, their three children, and then himself. "Nothing about God makes sense to me anymore," she wrote.

Theologian John Stott said, "The fact of suffering undoubtedly constitutes the single greatest challenge to the Christian faith, and has been in every generation. Its distribution and degree appear to be entirely random and therefore unfair."

The position many sufferers come to is not to deny God's

existence; it makes sense to believe in His existence. They also may not deny His sovereignty; it's obvious that He "works all things according to the counsel of His will" (Ephesians 1:11 NKJV). But when pain is "random and . . . unfair," the issue becomes the character of God. What kind of God would allow such suffering and seemingly do nothing to alleviate it?

As C. S. Lewis watched his wife suffer during her terminal illness, he said, "Not that I am in danger of ceasing to believe in God. The real danger is of coming to believe such dreadful things about Him. The conclusion I dread is not 'So, there's no God after all'; but 'So this is what God's really like.'"

Feeling abandoned by God is soul shattering. It raises the question of whether or not we have bought into a sentimental-ized package of God perpetuated by the Christian world intent on protecting His image. Is God truly involved with His cre-ation? Is that involvement motivated by the overwhelming love and compassion we were led to believe characterize His atti-tude toward us? Why do our experiences sometimes not coin-cide with that image? Why does He allow suffering?

Sooner or later in life our circumstances will force us to ask these questions. Admittedly, much about God will remain a mys-tery, but we can seek knowledge where it may be found. Faith requires some knowledge, and as we have already agreed, "blind faith" is not a requirement. So let's look to some facts that may strengthen our faith commitment even as we wonder about God.

When our son, Jeff, was around eight years old, he began attaching the word *evil* to everything he did not like. For instance, broccoli was evil, bedtime was evil, the playground supervisor was evil, and the supreme evil was a boy named

Timothy Drewsome who tyrannized the "little kids" in the neighborhood.

One evening Jeff and I were going through our bedtime ritual of chatting, reading a Bible story, and praying when Jeff startled me by saying he had decided God was evil. I had feared the evil labeling would one day extend beyond broccoli and was not sure what I'd say when that day came.

I asked him why he had decided God was evil. "Well, He made everything," Jeff mused, "so He made evil. If He had not made evil, Timothy Drewsome would not even be alive! That pretty much proves everything, Mom."

I must admit Timothy Drewsome showed an enormous degree of inherent depravity, but Jeff and I didn't talk about that. Instead I told him the origin of evil was the disobedience of Adam and Eve. That disobedience was their choice, not God's. Jeff huffed himself onto his left side, turned out the light, and said, "Mom, you blame them for everything!"

He was right. I do blame them for everything. Were it not for their self-centered narcissism, which insisted, "I'll do it my way," sin would not have ruined the perfect world God created. There would be no AIDS epidemic, my correspondent's family would not have been murdered by her clinically depressed son-in-law, and there would be no torture chambers, wars, devastating earthquakes, tornadoes, floods, or other calamities. Genesis 1:31 (NASB) records that when God finished creating the world, He "saw all that He had made, and behold, it was very good." So what happened to all that was good?

Adam and Eve were given the ability to make choices. They could make bad choices, or they could make good choices.

They could choose to be obedient to God's instruction, or they could bring on the onslaught of sin-consequence. They did not know disobedience would bring on sin-consequence; they didn't think that far ahead. They just knew the forbidden apple held a certain intrigue; they were curious, so they ate it! Then it hit them. They who had not yet experienced anything other than what was good suddenly recognized and experienced what was not good. They were ashamed. They hid from God. They knew then that He knew. They knew then that they knew. Innocence lost. Sin birthed.

> *God created a world in which people had*
> *genuine freedom and yet there was always*
> *the possibility to choose evil.*

The Adam and Eve account raises questions about God we need to think about. Obviously, God gave them free will, the ability to choose. They chose evil. But what was in their originally good nature that would even consider evil? What was its source? Did God create evil? How did they even think of disobedience if that propensity was not already there?

God is not the creator of evil. That would be totally against His divine nature. But built into the decision God made to give His creation freedom of choice was the chance of an evil choice. God created a world in which people had genuine freedom, and yet there was always the possibility to choose evil. That's what freedom is: I can choose good, or I can choose evil. Both opposites have to be present in order for a choice to be made.

For centuries scoffers have taken the fact of overriding evil in the world as evidence that God is not good. If He were, He would not allow evil to exist. Since it does, they say God is a bad God.

What the scoffers do not take into account is that when Adam and Eve chose sin, God honored their freedom to make that choice. If God used force to prevent their choice, He would have to remove all freedom of choice from that point on. The result would be little God robots programmed to do good. It would be, in essence, a forced good, a forced love, a forced relationship. Apparently God did not find that appealing. He wants His creation to choose to love Him, choose to know Him, and choose to seek Him with all their hearts. God is not a bad God; He is a relational God.

Others maintain (erroneously) that God does not stop the suffering because He can't. They say He is many things but He is not all-powerful. Rabbi Harold Kushner says in his bestseller *When Bad Things Happen to Good People*, "God isn't all-powerful. He would like to help, but He just isn't capable of solving all the problems in the world. . . . Even God has a hard time keeping chaos in check."

Believers discount this idea without even referencing the Bible; we see the evidence of an all-powerful God everywhere we look. Does it make sense that the solar system with all its scientific intricacies didn't stump God, but the messes we create do?

Another pivotal question about God's granting of free choice is this: Does God become the victim of our choices? Does He have to be subservient to the creatures to whom He granted these freedoms?

God is not scrambling to put Plan B in
place because my choice blew off Plan A.

One of the reasons I find such liberation in the doctrine of God's sovereignty is that not now, nor ever will He be subservient to my choices. I haven't a clue how He honors my choices and yet His plans prevail. That's a mystery. But nowhere in Scripture do we read about Plan B. God is not scrambling to put Plan B in place because my choice blew off Plan A.

So now we swing back to our original question: Why is there so much suffering and pain in life? Quite simply, when sin entered the world, so did the potential for all suffering: disease, murder, rape, etc. Though we hate the consequences of that choice, we can't blame God for the consequences. But we do. We blame Him.

When we blame God, we're guilty of faulty thinking. We want God to make exceptions for us in spite of the consequence of that original choice. When He does not, we question His compassion, we question His love, we question His commitment. Very quickly, our pain leads us to question His character, as did C. S. Lewis as he watched his wife die; as did the mother after the murder of her daughter and grandchildren; as do I as I watch the health struggles of Barbara Johnson and worry about the future of my little African heartthrob.

What are we thinking? We're thinking God should do things our way.

(That was Eve's thinking!)

Quite frankly, my way would be to keep myself exempt from sin-consequence. After all, I'm not the one who chose to disobey. I'm not the one who fell into conversation with a snake. I'd kill it with a garden hoe before I'd ever have a theological discussion about God's will and an apple. Mercy!

But wanting to present a reasonable face to God, I think, *OK, I'll take a little pain. It would make sense for me to have a little pain because of the Garden thing, but I don't think I should have very much.*

The reason I don't think I should have very much pain is because I've been a pretty good person. Let the pagans in the world get hefty doses of pain, but not me, not Barbara Johnson, not the mother who raised her children in the church, not my little heartthrob. I'll accept colitis, high blood pressure, and the annoyances of life like mosquitoes, people who make mouth noises, and my computer. I'll accept those imperfections without much carrying on. Keep it small, and I won't question God's character.

God's Determination to Demonstrate Love

Knowing suffering is a sin-consequence may be clarifying for my mind but little comfort for my soul. When I'm hurting, I don't want someone explaining the *why* to me. I want to know God truly loves me. I don't want a saccharine version. I want the real thing. Is His heart truly one of love and compassion in spite of how it appears? Having discussed His determination to give us freedom, let's now discuss His determination to demonstrate love.

*When I'm hurting, I don't want someone
explaining the "why" to me. I want to
know God truly loves me.*

Throughout Scripture, our faith object, we read that God's heart is full of love for His creation:

- Hosea 11:4 (NIV): "I led them with cords of human kindness, with ties of love."

- Jeremiah 31:3 (NIV): "I have loved you with an everlasting love."

- First John 4:10 (NIV): "This is love: not that we loved God, but that he loved us and sent his Son as an atoning sacrifice for our sins."

- John 3:16: "For God so loved the world . . ."

We also read that God the Father and Jesus the Son are One. That's why Jesus explained to His disciples in John 14:9–10 (NIV) that "anyone who has seen [Jesus] has seen the Father." Paul described Jesus as "the image of the invisible God" (Colossians 1:15 NIV). The writer of Hebrews referred to Jesus as the "exact representation" of God's being (1:3 NIV). When Jesus wept at the tomb of Lazarus . . . so did God. When Jesus invited the children to come to Him . . . that was God. The touch of Jesus restored sight, healed bodies, and renewed physical life . . . and that was also the touch of God.

Our faith is encouraged by knowing that the compassionate

acts of Jesus were the compassionate acts of God. He sits with us in our pain and refuses to leave us. He turns His ear toward our cries and listens until we're spent. Jesus hung on a cross for our sins and said, "It is finished!" (John 19:30). What started in the Garden was finished at the cross. The price was paid, the death sentence lifted.

What motivates such intense attention? Love. The love of God. The love of God demonstrated through the earthly ministrations of Jesus, God's Son.

The Old Testament prophet Micah said of God:

> Where is another God like you, who pardons the sins of the survivors among his people? You cannot stay angry with your people forever, because you delight in showing mercy. Once again you will have compassion on us. You will trample our sins under your feet and throw them into the depths of the ocean! You will show us your faithfulness and unfailing love as you promised with an oath to our ancestors Abraham and Jacob long ago. (7:18–20)

From the beginning of recorded time God has committed Himself to loving His people. He will continue loving His people until we all gather in that place called "eternity" where all tears will be wiped away, all pain will be eliminated, and all anguishing memories will be forgotten.

Choose Life

In the meantime, how do we cope with the problems pain presents to our faith? How do we maintain faith when suffering wrenches it from our feeble grasp? I go back to one of the free-doms given to me at creation: I choose.

I can choose to turn away from God in bitterness, despair, and disbelief, or I can choose to say, "Though He slay me, yet will I trust Him" (Job 13:15 NKJV).

Shortly before Moses died, he challenged the Hebrew people with these words: "Today I have given you the choice between life and death, between blessings and curses. . . . Oh, that you would choose life" (Deuteronomy 30:19).

What does it mean to choose life? It means to believe God's love for me is a dependable fact and in that love to find sustaining encouragement. It means I choose to live in the mystery of what I may not understand but feel buoyed by faith in the midst of that mystery. It means taking God's promises and believing they were written for me.

One such promise is Romans 8:28 (NKJV): "We know that all things work together for good to those who love God, to those who are the called according to His purpose." In choosing life, I choose to believe the enormous implications of that verse when I'm at my wits' end. We'll think about Romans 8:28 some more in the next chapter.

1. Why do you think God allows suffering when He is capable of preventing it?

2. Discuss a time in your life when God appeared to do nothing to help you. How did that affect your relationship with God?

3. What does Adam and Eve's disobedience in the Garden of Eden have to do with this world's suffering?

Faulty Thought No. 9:
God might be odd

Having stated my strongly held conviction that I choose to believe God's promises were written for me and that Romans 8:28 is one of those colossal promises, I'll tell you about one of my major experiences of shaky faith. It was accompanied by major faulty thinking. (As you remember, the two are usually in each other's company.)

This experience was the most dramatic "bring them out of their distresses" spiritual intervention I've ever had. Not only was it the most dramatic, it was the most memorably peculiar.

Years ago I was to drive my elderly parents from Sun City, Arizona, to Covenant Village in San Diego. Neither was in good health; we knew Covenant Village would be their last stopping place before heaven.

I felt anxious about their well-being as we anticipated the six-hour trip across the desert at temperatures over one hundred degrees. So, before leaving, Ken had our mechanic go over our car, looking for possible engine-trouble culprits. He replaced hoses and put on new tires. Then, because we had taken every precaution for safety, I left with confidence to pick up my parents in Arizona and bring them back to California.

I was relieved as we successfully made our way back through Yuma, Arizona, and headed into the last few hours of the return trip. My friend Darlene was with me, sitting next to Dad in the backseat; Mom sat in the front with me. All was going well. I thanked God for the peace and assurance I was beginning to feel.

I was amused as we approached a lonely sign by the side of the freeway; it read "Ocotillo, last chance for gas and food." As we approached Ocotillo and its look of utter desolation, I was relieved we had eaten and fueled in Yuma. I looked condescendingly over at what I assumed was Ocotillo and thought, *Thank You, Jesus, that I'm not going there!*

The thought no sooner left my mind when the car began to sputter and then spew steam. I lost all power: steering, brakes, and windows. The dashboard lights came on, complaining about everything. I coasted into Ocotillo.

There were two buildings: a closed gas station and an abandoned café. The café door swung listlessly back and forth on uncertain hinges. The stifling desert breeze made it difficult to breathe. It was eerie as I stuck my head in the door to see if anyone was alive inside. There was no one. I wasn't surprised. The entire population had died leaving no note.

The thermometer on the outside wall of the café registered 118 degrees. I panicked. *Lord Jesus, how could You! My parents have served You in ministry for over fifty years. Are You just going to let them shrivel up and die in this godforsaken spot? It might be reasonable for me to have a preview of hell, but not my parents!*

With the car door open, the four of us had a strategy meeting. Dad had noticed two vehicles by the side of the road about a quarter mile behind us. Darlene and I took off. My parents said they'd pray. *See, Lord? They're saints! How could You!*

As Darlene and I came closer to the two vehicles, I warned her that the drivers were probably slumped over the steering wheels dead. To our amazement, one of the vehicles was an AAA truck with a live driver.

Breathless and drenched with sweat, we approached the AAA truck, and I attempted to talk to the driver. He appeared not to see or hear me. I thought maybe he was dead after all. But he startled me by taking a long swig from his Coke can then answering my question: "Yep . . . I'm headin' fer San Diego."

"You're crazy, Marilyn. They don't want to help us . . . they'll rob us and kill us!"

Excitedly I pointed to my still-steam-spewing car off in the distance. I told him it was totally disabled and that my two elderly parents were not well either and asked if he could please tow us to San Diego. He slowly turned his head in the direction of my car, took another swig of Coke, and said, "I kin haul ya, but two of ya will have to ride with Cid." We, for the first time, turned our heads to view the other vehicle and take a good look at Cid. He too was taking periodic swigs from his Coke can. He did not look at either of us.

His car looked to be the finest vehicle Rent-A-Dent had to offer. It had multiple colors of paint, a barely attached front bumper, and was utterly filthy. I looked again at Cid. He looked like his car. Sighing, I said, "It's a deal."

As we huffed our way back to the car, Darlene said, "You're crazy, Marilyn. They don't want to help us . . . they'll rob us and kill us!"

"I know, I know," I replied. "But what choice do we have?

We could die if we stay here. We can at least take a chance with them. Maybe we'll outwit them before they kill us!"

In talking to my parents, they agreed we really had no option but to entrust ourselves to Tony (the AAA driver) and Cid (his Rent-A-Dent buddy). I drew Darlene aside and said, "OK, here's the plan. You go in the truck with Dad. You sit in the middle. If Tony takes an off-ramp heading for one of these little isolated roads where he'll try to kill you both, push him out of the truck, grab the wheel, and drive to San Diego. At all costs, you have to save my father."

"So what about you, Mrs. James Bond?"

"I'll put Mom in the front seat with Cid. The backseat is littered with empty bottles and trash, but I saw a wrench on the floor. I'm sitting in the back next to the wrench. The second he heads for an off-ramp, I'll hit him over the head with the wrench, push him out the door, and drive Mom to San Diego."

Cid was cleaning debris from the front seat to make room for my mother. As soon as she was settled, I crawled into the back within grabbing distance of the wrench. As Tony began hoisting my car up on its two hind tires, I nodded at Darlene as she seated Dad next to the door and herself in the middle. Plan in place.

Cid pulled out onto the freeway. Within minutes he headed for the first off-ramp. My hand reached for the wrench. Clutching it behind my back, I said, "Why are you getting off the freeway?"

Woodenly Cid responded, "We'll wait for Tony to go by . . . he needs gas."

That was stupid. Why hadn't Cid simply waited while Tony hoisted my car? Why wait here? Did he think I didn't know he planned to kill us?

Within minutes the AAA truck hauling Darlene, Dad, and my car passed by our spot on the side road. Cid muttered, "We'll follow 'em."

Duh! The sign pointing to Ocotillo said it was our last chance for gas. If the sign was accurate, there would be no hope of a gas station for miles. We all were moving toward our "last-chance" moment. I clutched the wrench more tightly.

To my utter amazement, a gas station soon became visible to the left of the freeway. It was not a mirage. We all pulled in. I put my wrench back in the pile of debris on the floor. Cid turned to my mother and asked in his mechanical voice if she would like a soft drink—a Coke, root beer, or Orange Crush. The word *Crush* seemed a bad omen to me. Cid brought Mom an ice-cold Orange Crush, which she drank gratefully.

As we all pulled out onto the freeway and made our uneventful way to San Diego, I took my eye off the wrench. No one had made a move to kill us. What was this about? Were we actually going to arrive at our destination safely? Cid had even asked my mother if she minded if he smoked. My ever-gracious mother said of course she did not mind. I minded! But he had not asked me. He cracked the little window (which was already cracked in several places) just enough to let the smoke escape from his cigarette. I could hardly smell it.

We eventually pulled into a Mobil station only a few miles from Covenant Village. Apparently my loquacious father had successfully started a conversation with Tony, who loved to fish. Since Dad was an avid fisherman, Darlene told me later, they exchanged fish stories crossing the arid and no longer hostile desert. Tony knew where Covenant Village was as well as the location of this Mobil station, which had a mechanic on duty. It was an effortless "drop-off" for everyone instead of the knockoff I had expected. Amazing!

I called Covenant Village, which immediately sent a representative to pick up my parents. Seeing them safely on their way, I turned to Tony, who was gently lowering my car to the ground. With checkbook in hand I walked over to him and asked what I owed. I had muttered to myself earlier that though these two rough-looking fellows were apparently not going to murder us, I was sure I'd be charged an outrageous price for the tow, which Cid and Tony would gleefully share with each other later.

Expressionlessly he said, "A hundred bucks."

I was stunned.

"Tony, that isn't enough. That's only a dollar a mile," I told him and then waited for a response. Finally he said, "I was comin' this way anyway . . . no problem to me." I suddenly wanted to hug him. I wanted to tell him how wonderfully kind he had been to us and how easily he could have simply driven off and left us in Ocotillo, but he had chosen to help us instead. I wrote a check for a much larger amount than he'd asked. As I handed it to him, he didn't look at me or the check. He stuffed it into his pocket and walked over to talk to the mechanic on duty. I said softly to his retreating back, "You saved our lives, Tony . . . thank you so much." He didn't respond.

God did a Romans 8:28 on me.
I did not fully understand it until it was all over.

Cid was sitting motionlessly behind the wheel of his "Rent-A-Dent." I walked over to his window and tried to hand him some cash. He brushed it away and said, "I was comin' anyway . . . no problem to me."

I was starting to feel pretty weepy about this experience, so I simply patted Cid's dirty, T-shirted shoulder and told him he was a gift from God. That must have startled him, because I successfully dropped the cash into his car and walked away before he had a chance to give it back.

God's Ways May Be . . . Weird

While Darlene and I waited for my car to be fixed, I asked her if she thought Cid and Tony might be angels. Admittedly they were peculiar, bad-looking, and one of them smoked, but how did they just happen to be in Ocotillo at the very moment we needed them? And how did it happen that the two things we needed to get us out of Ocotillo were two vehicles—a tow truck and a passenger car—and there they were, parked by the side of the road, seemingly waiting just for us? What was that all about?

God did a Romans 8:28 on me. I did not fully understand it until it was all over. Why was it so difficult to grasp? I fell victim to some faulty thinking that tangled with my faith. These were my thoughts:

- *We have been abandoned by God in Ocotillo.*

- *Someone has got to do something. I guess that someone is me!*

- *These are bad-looking men whose only motive is to kill us, rob us, and leave our bodies to shrivel up in the heat.*

- *The only recourse we have to save ourselves is violence: shove Tony . . . hit Cid.*

- *I'll drop my faith and pick up a wrench.*

My faulty thinking was a problem to my faith in yet another way. I know faith is believing God, whom I cannot see but in whom I've chosen to put my trust no matter how things appear. But everything appeared to be so weird. The men were weird, Ocotillo was weird, my supposedly healthy car was even weird.

My faith didn't seem able to extend to weird. Well, guess what: God does extend to weird. First Corinthians 1:27–29 states,

> God deliberately chose things the world considers foolish in order to shame those who think they are wise. And he chose those who are powerless to shame those who are powerful. God chose things despised by the world, things counted as nothing at all, and used them to bring to nothing what the world considers important, so that no one can ever boast in the presence of God.

I love this reminder about God's ways, but I never once thought of it in Ocotillo. He says, "My ways are far beyond anything you could imagine" (Isaiah 55:8), but I guess for some dumb reason I think His ways should be a little more recog-nizable. In choosing "things despised by the world" (i.e., Cid, Tony, Ocotillo), God totally succeeded in confounding me. His purpose is to make "all things work together for good" in ways that would never occur to me, and He works things in ways that reflect His unmistakable style. For example, if we had not experienced mechanical trouble, we would have shimmered our way across the desert grateful for a good car instead of a creative God.

You can understand my need to have a "come to Jesus" chat as soon as everything was settled and I'd returned home to Ken, the kids, and the dog. When God and I were alone, I asked forgiveness for my brutal plan for Cid if he "got out of line." I expressed deep regret that my faith seemed to evaporate in the scorching desert air, leaving only my parched soul and a wad of fear.

I claimed Philippians 1:6 for myself during that sweet time of talking with my Father: "I am sure that God, who began the good work within you, will continue his work until it is finally finished on that day when Christ Jesus comes back again."

He did not judge my frail faith and faulty thoughts or my wits'-end mentality. He reminded me I'm still under construction and there's no way He'll quit until the job's done. I hate that it'll take a lifetime, but that apparently doesn't put God off.

1. Discuss a time when God was working for you, but you didn't recognize it because it didn't make sense to you.

2. What do you think about angels? Is it possible that they could be on this earth and we don't realize it? Can you discuss such a time in your own life?

3. What is the meaning of 1 Corinthians 1:29, which says, "So that no one can ever boast in the presence of God"? How would we boast?

Faulty Thought No. 10:
Someone else has an easier life

Have you ever thought life might be easier if you could completely change who you are or be someone else altogether? Here's one woman's fantasy for her own identity change: she'd like to be a bear. Her reasons?

- If you are a bear you get to hibernate; you do nothing but sleep for six months.

- Before you hibernate, you must eat huge amounts of food—the more calories the better.

- The children (cubs) are born while you are sleeping and are the size of walnuts. When you wake up they are already partially grown.

- As a mama bear, you swat anyone who bothers your cubs. Swatting is socially acceptable behavior.

- Your mate expects you to wake up growling and have hairy legs and excess body fat.

I thought of these bear "advantages" when I received a letter from a fourteen-year-old girl who told me she "pretty much" hated her mother and "pretty much" never saw her father. She wanted to move into her girlfriend's home because her girlfriend's mother was "cool." The fourteen-year-old asked for my opinion.

Though I didn't say this, I thought she might discover that the "cool" mother, in reality, had hairy legs and carried excess body fat that made her cranky. The result? Possible swatting.

Life is not perfect. We know that, but we still suspect someone else's life might be a little less imperfect than our own. We suspect other people's circumstances are far more manageable than ours, and often we wish we could just trade places with the persons we envy.

When my father took two years out of the ministry and bought forty acres of the most remote property on the face of the earth, I thought I'd die. Dad needed a people break. I didn't. I was nine years old and extremely social. There was no one to play with because there were no human beings near us.

Wilma Brownell's life was far preferable to me than my own. She lived "in town," had a few neighbors, and the little grocery store was right across the street. She could sit on the steps of the store and drink Pepsi from a bottle. I longed to sit on the grocery store steps and drink Pepsi from a bottle too.

Years later, I learned her father was alcoholic and abusive. She thought my life was ideal because during my two-year "Lonely Acres" era, I had the freedom to run and play with my dog, King, ride my bike to the bookmobile every two weeks, and then read those books in the leaf-enshrouded tree house I'd built with my very own hands. Wilma and I thought each other's life looked perfect.

The longing for perfection has always been with us. Why? We were created for perfection. How else does one explain looking for what we've never known? When perfection was lost in the Garden of Eden, expectation was not lost. We live hoping for what we've never known, somehow knowing one day it will be ours. The good news is, perfection is on its way. One day all evil will be banished, taking with it all that is not perfect.

Romans 8:28 is a good-news verse. It does not promise perfection but provides optimism for what we hope will be the outcome of our experiences. It says, "All things work together for good to those who love God, to those who are the called according to His purpose" (NKJV). We latch onto the thought that all things work together for good because we are desperate for perfection. Most of us have lives that are far from perfect. There is truth in Henry Thoreau's statement: "Most people live lives of quiet desperation." We want God to put everything together again, make it good so we can quit envying everyone else's life, and get on with our own.

When Our Deliverance Doesn't Work Out as Expected

The reason I want to take an additional look at Romans 8:28 is because many of us get to a wits'-end experience, cry out, claim Romans 8:28, and then become disillusioned because the deliverance from all our distresses promised in Psalm 107:27–28—the "working together for good"—does not work out as we expected.

He has a purpose I may not understand or
even imagine, but in His time and in His way,
His purpose will be accomplished.

There is a key phrase in the Romans 8:28 verse that is crucial for us to consider: "called according to His purpose." We remember God is in complete charge of all the events in our lives. He's not only in charge of the events, He is also in charge of the timing. He has a purpose I may not understand or even imagine, but in His time and in His way, His purpose will be accomplished.

Let's take a look at Jacob in the Old Testament. How God worked a Romans 8:28 on him, his sons, and ultimately the nation of Israel is one of the most fascinating stories in Scripture. You may remember, Jacob was the father of Joseph, whose brothers first tried to kill him but opted later to sell him into slavery instead.

As a young man, before having a wife and kids, Jacob had a dramatic experience with God. Genesis 28 says Jacob lay down to sleep and dreamed about a ladder that was "set up on the earth, and its top reached to heaven" and "the angels of God were ascending and descending on it" (v. 12 NKJV).

When Jacob woke up from his dream, he said, "Surely the LORD is in this place, and I did not know it" (v. 16 NKJV). Here is where the majority of us can chime in with Jacob and say, "I did not know it." God is everyplace: He is everywhere, but so often we don't know it. God is indeed working out His purposes. That's what He does, and He does it in our presence, whether or not we know it.

> *God is everyplace: He is everywhere,*
> *but so often we don't know it.*

The night of Jacob's dream God spoke personally to him: "Behold, I am with you and will keep you wherever you go, and will bring you back to this land; for I will not leave you until I have done what I have spoken to you" (v. 15 NKJV).

Wouldn't you think after that tailor-made, personal promise from the God of the universe, Jacob's faith would never falter? Well, it did falter. It faltered to the point where, in despair, he said, "Everything is going against me!" (Genesis 42:36). How could Jacob think everything was going against him when God Himself had promised to be with him wherever he went?

Jacob's memory of God's promise began to recede as his life played out. As an old man, Jacob had a favorite son named Joseph. Joseph's brothers told their father Joseph had been killed by wild animals. They dipped Joseph's coat in animal blood and showed it to Jacob to support their lie. Jacob was heartbroken. He did not know God's purpose was being worked out exactly as He had promised in that dream years ago.

Let's skip ahead in the story of Joseph, Jacob's son, and see the working of God's purpose in his life. Here are the highlights:

- Joseph was sold to Egyptian slave traders, who in turn sold him to Potiphar, a high-ranking official in the Egyptian government. In time Joseph was put in charge of Potiphar's entire household.

- Potiphar's wife found Joseph attractive and made a move on him. When she was rebuffed by Joseph, she falsely accused Joseph of the very move she herself had instigated. Joseph was thrown in jail.

- Joseph earned the respect of the jailer, who put Joseph in charge of all the prisoners.

- Joseph was called from jail to successfully interpret Pharaoh's troubling and prophetic dream. Joseph was then elevated to the second-highest position in Egypt. In addition, he was named administrator of "Famine Preparation."

Amid the account of Joseph's story (in Genesis 37–50), including the many personal calamities Joseph suffered, we find these words: "The Lord was with him." God's purpose was being accomplished in spite of all appearances, and the Lord never left him.

The severe famine struck Egypt and the neighboring nations just as Pharaoh had dreamed and as Joseph had interpreted. Jacob sent his sons to Egypt to seek supplies. Because of Joseph's wise leadership, food and grain were stored in Egypt in anticipation of the famine.

When Joseph's brothers came to the royal court, they did not recognize their brother. He was dressed in the clothing of a royal official and spoke to them through an interpreter. Joseph recognized *them*, however, but pretended he did not.

Joseph accused them of being spies. He put them in prison, except for one brother who was instructed to go home and return with Benjamin, the youngest brother. This was frightening to the brothers because their traitorous deeds of years earlier against Joseph came flooding back on their consciences. "They said to one another, 'Surely we are being punished because of our brother. We saw how distressed he was when he pleaded with us for his life, but we would not listen; that's why this distress has come upon us'" (Genesis 42:21 NIV).

Reuben, the oldest brother, said, "Didn't I tell you not to sin against the boy? But you wouldn't listen! Now we must give an accounting for his blood" (v. 22 NIV).

The years of "keeping up appearances" with their father and perpetuating the lie that Joseph had been killed by wild animals had now backfired on them. They knew they were going to be punished.

After a number of tension-producing tests Joseph devised, including planting incriminating evidence in the grain sacks the brothers were carrying back home, Joseph revealed who he really was. In addition to revealing who he was, he told his brothers God's purpose in all that had happened to him:

> Do not be distressed and do not be angry with your-selves for selling me here, because it was to save lives that God sent me ahead of you. For two years now there has been famine in the land, and for the next five years there will not be plowing and reaping. But God sent me ahead of you to preserve for you a remnant on earth and to save your lives by a great deliverance.
>
> So then, it was not you who sent me here, but God. (Genesis 45:5–8 NIV)

But the brothers were terrified and still expected punishment for their sin against Joseph. Instead, he underscored all he had told them by saying, "You intended to harm me, but God intended it for good to accomplish what is now being done, the saving of many lives" (Genesis 50:20 NIV).

Not only were lives saved as a result of Joseph's painful journey to prominence, but God's promise to Jacob was honored as well. When Jacob left his homeland, God told him there would be an ultimate return to it, which God would orchestrate.

When Pharaoh invited all of Joseph's family to come to Egypt, God appeared again to Jacob, saying, "I am God, the God of your father; do not fear to go down to Egypt, for I will make of you a great nation there. I will go down with you to Egypt, and I will also surely bring you up again" (Genesis 46:3–4 NKJV).

God did, indeed, bring Jacob's descendants back to their Promised Land, but not without the passing of time, confusing circumstances, and seemingly no hope of all things working together for good. But that good was exactly as God ordained it. First Chronicles 29:12 (NIV) reminds us, "In your hands are strength and power to exalt and give strength to all." God purposed to give strength and then power to Joseph, who in turn gave strength and power to his people living in Egypt. The descendants of those people would one day become the nation of Israel.

God's Purpose and God's Ordained Good

Romans 8:28 is about God's purpose. It is not necessarily about what looks good, feels good, or is even remotely attractive. Although there is no scriptural indication that Joseph complained about his circumstances, it would be under-standable if he had wanted to trade places with anyone if it meant being freed from slavery or jail so he could then go home to his family. But Joseph learned that with God's pur-pose, there was also God's ordained good. I'm convinced that when we can truly understand that truth, we may be less resistant to the ordained good we can't see.

> *I'm convinced that when we can truly*
> *understand that truth, we may be less resistant*
> *to the ordained good we can't see.*

Carol Kent, popular Christian speaker and author, experienced the most horrendously heart-wrenching circumstance I can imagine. Her son Jason was arrested for murder. It didn't make sense. Jason was one of those wonderfully perfect kids. He was a graduate of the U.S. Naval Academy and was preparing to leave for his first military assignment in Hawaii. He'd served as president of the National Honor Society, worked with Habitat for Humanity, gone on mission trips, and was deeply commit-ted to his faith.

But in front of witnesses, Jason fatally shot his wife's ex-husband, who allegedly had sexually abused their children. When the court had approved the ex-husband's petition to have private visitations with the two little girls, Jason became extremely agitated; something inside him snapped. He wanted to protect the children from their father. Now Jason was con-victed of first-degree murder and sentenced to life in prison. He was twenty-seven.

Carol writes about the experience in her new book, *When I Lay My Isaac Down*. Everything about this story breaks my heart, but one particularly gut-wrenching section of the book describes the emotions Carol experienced when she visited Jason for the first time in jail. She said he walked down the hall into the visitation area in handcuffs. He had a chain around his waist to which the handcuffs were linked, and leg irons that made it difficult to walk. He'd been badly beaten by others in the prison; his front teeth were broken off, and his eye was bloodshot from the beating. Separated by a Plexiglas partition, they both sobbed. Everything now was totally beyond their control.

But what God is doing now with the Kents is rather amazing, unless of course one does not believe in Romans 8:28. From this rubble of pain has emerged a new and unique ministry called "Speak Up for Hope." The goal is to connect churches and organizations with nearby prisons. These groups then work with the prison chaplains in an effort to bring hope and help to inmates and their families.

The organization is also working to network educators with prison chaplains in order to provide GED programs and marriage-and-family classes. An effort is being made to connect business professionals to soon-to-be-released inmates who will need job information.

In all of this is Jason, who is an assistant to the prison chaplain. His desire is to be used in any way God sees fit; his faith and commitment are still strong. It would appear that he and his parents are experiencing the "all things" principle. I respect and admire them enormously.

What about Eve?

Both Joseph in the Old Testament and Carol in our present day were able to see at least a portion of God's sovereign purpose when He took evil and brought good from it. But what about Eve? (Remember the woman from Eden?) Did she ever see the working out of God's purpose from her original sin? Can we imagine God doing a Romans 8:28 on the woman who got the whole ball of sin rolling?

Of course we can, although it may be a new thought to contemplate. Though Eve was the original sinner, we all carry her mark. (I know Adam was equally responsible, but I'm just going to talk about Eve for a minute. She, like us, was a part of God's grand plan, as the following passage from Isaiah reminds us.)

> *This is the plan determined for the whole world;*
> *this is the hand stretched out over all nations.*
> *For the LORD Almighty has purposed, and who can*
> *thwart him?*
> *His hand is stretched out, and who can turn it back?*
> *(14:26–27 NIV)*

The authority of God was not unknown to Eve. She experienced it the minute she and her wimp-husband were caught in their buck-passing explanation to God about their disobedience:

> "Have you eaten from the tree that I commanded you not to eat from?"

The man said, "The woman you put here with me—
she gave me some fruit from the tree, and I ate it." . . .

The woman said, "The serpent deceived me, and I
ate." (Genesis 3:11–13 NIV)

God then passed judgment upon their disobedience:

So the LORD God banished [Adam] from the Garden of
Eden to work the ground from which he had been
taken. After he drove the man out, he placed on the east
side of the Garden of Eden cherubim and a flaming
sword flashing back and forth to guard the way to the
tree of life. (3:23–24 NIV)

Neither Adam nor Eve could have imagined God had a
"plan determined for the whole world," which their disobedience flung into place. All they could see was the immediate.
They blew it and were evicted. I'm sure if Eve were not the
only person around, she would have loved to change places
with whomever. The problem was, there *were* no whomevers.

Soon they had two sons, Cain and Abel. In a fit of jealous
rage, Cain murdered his brother, Abel. How could all things
work together for good here? How could God's purpose be
accomplished with this motley crew?

As He had done with Adam, God confronted Cain. God
asked him where his brother was. With sullen disrespect, Cain
said, "Am I my brother's keeper?" Cain, like his father, Adam,
was then banished from his land. Cain was condemned to be
a "restless wanderer on the earth" (Genesis 4:9, 12 NIV).

All things have a purpose as they accomplish God's will.

Now, of course Romans 8:28 had not been written at the time of Adam and Eve, but the principle resides in the very nature of God. There never was, nor will there ever be, a time when God does not operate out of His basic principle. What is the principle?

All things . . . His will.

In addition, all things have a purpose as they accomplish God's will.

Could Eve have known that? Did she see God's principle working in her life? We can see now, from our perspective, how God's purpose was accomplished, but I think it's safe to say that she was one person who never had the assurance of all things working together for good in terms of her earthly circumstances. But in terms of God's plan for the whole world, we all, in spite of earthly circumstances, are elevated to a place of being loved and revered by the God who put everything into motion from the beginning. "Long before he laid down earth's foundations, he had us in mind, had settled on us as the focus of his love. . . . Long, long ago he decided to adopt us into his family through Jesus Christ" (Ephesians 1:4–5 MSG).

This is good news not only for us but for Adam and Eve as well. Knowing they would bring sin into the world, they were still the focus of God's love. With that loving assurance, I don't think I will have need of trading places with anyone I envy.

1. What kinds of people do you most envy? Why is there envy?

2. What does the phrase "called according to His purpose" mean for your life? Is that a comforting phrase? Why?

3. What is God's ultimate purpose for every life?

I need to hide my feelings from God

A passenger in a taxi leaned over to ask the driver a question and tapped him on the shoulder. The driver screamed, lost control of the cab, nearly hit a bus, drove up over the curb, and stopped just inches from a large plate-glass window.

For a few moments everything was silent in the cab, then the still-shaking driver said, "I'm sorry, but you scared me to death."

The frightened passenger apologized to the driver and said he didn't realize a mere tap on the shoulder could scare him so much.

The driver replied, "No, no, I'm sorry. It's entirely my fault. It's just that today is my first day driving a cab. . . . I've been driving a hearse for the last twenty-five years."

Sometimes we act as if God might be like that cabdriver. Were we to tell Him how we really feel, He might be so startled and horrified by what we say He'd jump the curb and hit a light pole.

Now, of course we understand in our rational minds that God knows everything we think. *The Message* translation of Psalm 139:2 says, "I'm an open book to you; even from a distance, you know what I'm thinking." Depending on how comfortable we are with being an "open book," we may like the fact we're so thoroughly known, or on the other hand, we may feel busted. A torrent of self-justification may follow the busted realization: *"Lord, I didn't really think that thought for more than a minute . . . or two." "I didn't really mean any of that stuff about hurting my husband; I think my blood sugar was low." "Well, yes, there are times when I question whether or not You are even hearing me. Of course I know You are, but . . . well . . . it doesn't feel like it. Nothing has changed. It isn't as if I've lost my faith in You . . . It's just You don't seem very present. I know I'll feel better in the morning. Please don't hold these thoughts against me."*

Honest Communication with God

David, writer of the Psalms, did not tiptoe around God out of fear that God would judge him, reject him, or hold his thoughts against him. David whined, fussed, and praised, depending on how he felt and what his circumstances were. He was secure in his relationship with God.

He was also secure in being totally authentic with God. Why? He believed with all his heart that God was committed to him. But David was human, and his faith wobbled when things were going badly. When circumstances were not in his favor, David second-guessed whether God really was committed to him after all. But, unlike many of us, David did not hide his feelings from God. In fact, David modeled for us the kind of honest communication it is possible to have with God, the kind that trusts God to receive our feelings and not judge us for having them.

One of the most startlingly honest psalms is 88. We read it and wonder, *How dare you say that stuff to God! Can you really just come out and tell Him you're begging for help and He seems to be ignoring you? Is it OK to say many of your prayers feel as if they fall on deaf ears? Isn't talking to God like that disrespectful?*

Let's refresh our memory on this psalm. As you read it, can you imagine feeling safe enough with God to be this real with Him?

> *O LORD, God of my salvation,*
> *I have cried out to you day and night.*
> *Now hear my prayer;*
> *listen to my cry.*
> *For my life is full of troubles,*
> *And death draws near. . . .*
> *I am forgotten,*
> *cut off from your care.*
> *You have thrust me down to the lowest pit,*
> *into the darkest depths.*
> *Your anger lies heavy on me;*
> *wave after wave engulfs me. . . .*
> *My eyes are blinded by my tears.*
> *Each day I beg for your help, O LORD;*
> *I lift my pleading hands to you for mercy. . . .*
> *O LORD, I cry out to you.*
> *I will keep on pleading day by day.*
> *O LORD, why do you reject me?*
> *Why do you turn your face away from me?*
> *(88:1–7, 9, 13–14)*

But then David said in Psalm 91:1–2, "Those who live in the shelter of the Most High will find rest in the shadow of the Almighty. This I declare of the LORD: He alone is my refuge, my place of safety; he is my God, and I am trusting him."

He expressed his regained peace in Psalm 94:17–18:

> *Unless the LORD had helped me,*
> *I would soon have died.*
> *I cried out, "I'm slipping!"*
> *and your unfailing love, O LORD, supported me.*

David and his emotions were all over the map, and God went all over the map with him. Remember, God is at our wits' end with us. He has said, "Never will I leave you; never will I forsake you" (Hebrews 13:5 NIV). When our backs are against the wall, God shares the wall. He shares the wall, not because He has no idea how to bring us out of our distresses, but because He is where we are . . . at the wall. His purpose will be accomplished in His time and in His way.

When our backs are against the wall, God shares the wall.

Learning to Cry Out Honestly to God

Some years ago I had a client named Amy whose eighteen-year-old son was hit and killed by a drunk driver. Amy was referred to me by a psychiatrist who wisely put her on an anti-depressant. Since she was a Christian, he thought I could help her.

She told me she had totally lost her enthusiasm for life. Her son, Stan, was all she had. She had been divorced early in the marriage, had no other children, and both her parents had died of cancer some time earlier. Humanly speaking, she truly was alone.

After a few sessions, I asked her to talk to me about her view of God and how she talked to Him about Stan's death. At first she looked a little frightened but then assured me she had faith in God; she knew Stan was with Him, and one day they would be together.

I asked her again to describe how she talked to God. She said though she still believed in Him, she wasn't talking to Him. She didn't know what to say if she did talk to Him. She also was afraid that if she ever got started talking, she'd lose it and say things she would then regret. After a long silence, she finally said, "You know, I was always taught to respect authority."

That translated to me that she probably had had a dictatorial parent who did not allow her to express herself. (In time I learned she was terrified of her father's coldly autocratic ways; she determined early in her life to hold her tongue and keep the peace.)

For some time we worked on the contrast between her father's ways and her heavenly Father's ways. One of my most gratifying experiences as a counselor was the morning when she was finally able to envision Jesus gathering her up as described in Mark 10:16: "He took the children into his arms and placed his hands on their heads and blessed them."

She cried long-pent-up tears as she experienced for the first time that she was tenderly and genuinely loved, that God's desire was to hold her in His arms and to bless her, not to criticize her or reject her.

Shortly after this sweet breakthrough, she began writing letters to God. She still was hesitant to hear the sound of her own voice addressing Him; it was easier to write to Him than to talk to Him. I asked her to read Psalm 88 as often as she was able and to envision in the psalmist's cry her own anger that her life was "full of troubles, and death draws near," that it felt as if God had forgotten her, cut her off from His care, thrust her "into the darkest depths," and that her eyes were "blinded by her tears."

That psalm ultimately released her feelings on several levels. To begin with, she realized she would not be struck dead if she told God how she felt. Second, she realized what a release it was for her to fully express her feelings. She didn't know how mad she was at God, but the fact that she could tell Him how she felt was liberating to her spirit as well as her mind.

She cried the pain and loss of her son until she was sure she had no more tears. But within hours, she was at it again. Each time she prayed her pain, she envisioned herself in the arms of Jesus, and He blessed her again and again with His faithful presence.

Amy never "got over" the loss of Stan in the sense that the hurt went away and the hole in her soul filled in. A deep loss remains just that: a deep loss. But she is functioning again and has an urgent desire to be an encouragement to others who have lost a son or daughter. She will never be the same; life will never be as it was. There is, however, an undergirding of strength she'd never known how to access. She learned God was with her at her wits' end; she also learned how to "cry out." To do so was to be honest with God.

Crying out is verbalizing our feelings. Crying out may be cutting loose from all the restraints we thought we had to maintain in order to be spiritually pleasing to God. All that restraint does is shut us down from ourselves and shut us off from God.

We don't have to pretend to believe Romans 8:28
at a time when it is totally unbelievable. God knows
the moment when that is too great a stretch.

We cry out for our sakes, not for God's sake. He already knows what we're feeling. But we tell Him what we're feeling for the good of our relationship with Him.

Humanly we feel close to the person who knows us, loves us, and does not judge us. We feel close to the one with whom we can really let our hair down. We're lucky when we have a close earthly friend we can share all our thoughts with. But there's no luck involved in having a divine Friend who offers this kind of solace and understanding. It's God! And He has promised to be with us and love us forever. We don't have to pretend to believe Romans 8:28 at a time when it is totally unbelievable. God knows the moment when that is too great a stretch. If we tell Him, we don't create a distance between us. We don't have to be a phony spiritual person, afraid to admit the need to cry out with David, "I'm going down to the pit; I'm a person without strength" (Psalm 88:4, my paraphrase). We can be our honest selves with God.

I love the words of that old hymn:

Just as I am, without one plea
But that Thy blood was shed for me,
And that Thou bidd'st me come to Thee,
O Lamb of God I come! I come!

How do we come to God? Just as we are. It was fifteen years ago that I worked with Amy in my counseling office. What a privilege it was to walk her path with her and watch her find her way to a renewed faith. I have a graduate degree in counseling psychology, and I deeply respect the field. But psychology does not heal; God does. Psychology gives us many valuable tools, but God gives grace-laced regeneration. It is the combination of what we know about psychology and what we believe about God that provides an effective formula for healing change. Amy's life is a perfect example of that.

Finding Our Home in God

When Joani was born with spina bifida, I had no background or understanding of what it meant to be honest with God, to tell Him my feelings as a child talking to her trusted Father. I thought if I did not present to God an image of one with unwavering faith, I would lose His favor . . . Joani would not be healed . . . and if she died it would be because I hadn't "believed better."

Now, years later, I realize my agitation was increased as I attempted to carry my own burden in the name of faith. If I had "cried out," would that have made a difference in Joani's life expectancy? I don't believe that to be true at all. But I do believe God would have received my crying out and given me a peace I did not have initially. I needed a place to go and break down emotionally. What better place than in the arms of Jesus, who would hold me, receive me, and bless me.

There is a homelessness of the self we impose upon ourselves when we don't realize it is God who is our home.

There is a homelessness of the self we impose upon ourselves when we don't realize it is God who is our home. We know believers anticipate a mansion in heaven, but here on earth God is also our home.

It is He who provides the comforts of home, which are far more than a nice paint job and a few throw pillows. These comforts are the security of being adored—nurtured and comforted, approved of and cherished—as He walks our human path with us. The home I'm talking about is that interior space within all of us where God lives. But we become like a homeless person if we don't recognize that haven within. When I was desperate in my prayers for Joani, I behaved like a homeless person, one who had no place to go. It's as if I stayed on a park bench and simply gritted my teeth for faith and healing for my baby. Since God is wherever I am, He shared the park bench with me, but there was a better place to be. There was a place that offered shelter, but I didn't seem to know it.

I believe many of us are afraid to cry out because we think to do so would alienate us from God. The result of that faulty thinking is that we don't go home, where honesty is rewarded and faith is increased. We stay in a homeless state, perhaps toughing it out on a park bench somewhere. What we need to do is cry out in the comfort of home.

Remember, home is that interior place in our spirits where God speaks words of encouragement to us. It's where He soothes our tattered souls and promises comfort. Isaiah 66:13 (NIV) says, "As a mother comforts her child, so will I comfort you." Home is that place where I can be real . . . where I can be honest . . . where I dare to say what I feel. It is hard to imagine how one could leave this interior home when we carry it within us. But it is possible to close the door to that home and walk away. I've done it. Many of us don't even know we do it. But it happens the moment we, with tight-lipped determination, try to carry our own burdens, work out our own solutions, and remain stoic in the process.

Revelation 3:20 (NIV) gives us an image of our interior home when we've walked away from it. This is what God says to us then:

> Here I am! I stand at the door and knock. If anyone hears my voice and opens the door, I will come in and eat with him, and he with me.

When I open the door, I've come home, and He is there. What do we then do? We celebrate with a great meal!

1. To what degree are you authentic with God? Do you generally hide your feelings from Him? If so, why?

2. If you tell God you feel weak, will that be a sign you lack faith? If you lack faith, will He still be pleased with you?

3. Why do you need to tell God what's really going on in your emotions? What's the advantage of that honesty?

I have too many doubts to be a Christian

A man was being tailgated by an uptight, stressed-out woman on a busy street. When the light suddenly turned yellow, the man stopped. He could have beaten the red light by accelerating through the intersection, but he chose to do the safer thing and stop. The tailgating woman hit her horn, rolled down her window, and screamed that the man had caused her to miss getting through the intersection

As she was still yelling and screaming, she heard a tap on the passenger-side window. It was a very serious-looking police officer. He ordered her to exit the car with her hands up.

He took her to the police station, where she was searched, fingerprinted, photographed, and placed in a cell. After a few hours another policeman approached the cell and escorted her back to the booking desk, where the arresting officer was waiting with her personal belongings.

He said, "I'm so sorry about this mistake. You see, I pulled up behind your car while you were leaning on your horn, giving the man in front of you significant finger gestures, and cussing a blue streak at him. When I saw the 'Choose Life' license plate holder, the 'What Would Jesus Do?' decal, the 'Follow Me to Sunday School' bumper sticker, and the chrome-plated Christian fish emblem, I just assumed you must have stolen the car."

What do you think was going on with this woman? Was she simply one who didn't "walk the talk"? Was she a rage-aholic who cut loose only behind the steering wheel but never in church?

Here's my take on her behavior. She obviously had an anger problem, an impulse-control problem, and a major behavior inconsistency between the messages plastered all over her car and her actions. But I ask, with deliberate "*pun*niness," what's behind all that? What's the underlying problem?

When We're Plagued with Doubts

Now I say, in all seriousness, when our behavior is so totally contrary to what we claim to believe, there's a possible problem with our belief system. Do we really, at the core of our being, believe what we say we believe? If our behavior does not reflect our beliefs, we are either well-practiced phonies or possibly persons plagued with doubts about what we claim to believe. More than likely we are both. The person who struggles with major doubts about her beliefs also struggles with her behavior because the two don't mesh; there isn't a fit. We think, *This is how I'm supposed to believe, but sometimes I don't think I believe any of it.* These doubts affect not only our peace but our actions.

Several weeks ago I received a letter from a woman who was afraid her many doubts would keep her out of heaven. She received Jesus as her Savior in her early twenties, married a Christian man, attends church regularly, and is active in her church's women's group. But she said she frequently wonders if the whole "God story" is true. Sometimes it sounds as far-fetched as a Hans Christian Andersen fairy tale. She especially struggles with the resurrection story; it is a major stretch for her to believe it. On the other hand, she is terrified of the possible consequences of having so many doubts. She wants to be a Christian, and her fear that maybe she really is not has caused her problems with depression. Her question of me was, Can a person struggle with doubt and still be a Christian?

A young friend of mine confessed similar doubts when she admitted she was bored in church, found the Bible difficult to understand, and her mind roamed all over the place when she prayed. She feared she might not be a Christian. How can a real Christian be bored out of her mind with everything that has to do with being a Christian? Did Jesus really come into her heart and life when she asked Him to? Did she maybe miss a step or two in the process? Will she make it to heaven?

The Bible clearly states the "right steps" we take to be sure we are heaven-bound when we die. Let's refresh our minds on those steps:

1. God's plan is that you know you are loved and that He created you so that you might know Him personally:

   God so loved the world that He gave His only begotten Son, that whoever believes in Him should not perish but have everlasting life. (John 3:16 NKJV)

   This is eternal life, that they may know You, the only true God, and Jesus Christ whom You have sent. (John 17:3 NKJV)

2. The way we can know God personally is to receive Jesus Christ as Savior.

As many as received Him, to them He gave the right to become children of God, to those who believe in His name. (John 1:12 NKJV)

Behold, I stand at the door and knock. If anyone hears My voice and opens the door, I will come in to him. (Revelation 3:20 NKJV)

3. The Bible promises eternal life (heaven) to all who receive Christ.

This is the testimony: that God has given us eternal life, and this life is in His Son. He who has the Son has life; he who does not have the Son of God does not have life. These things I have written to you who believe in the name of the Son of God, that you may know that you have eternal life, and that you may continue to believe in the name of the Son of God. (1 John 5:11–13 NKJV)

These verses tell us the only way to heaven is to know Jesus, God's Son, as our Savior. If we have received Him, we're heaven-bound. If we have not, then there's always the opportunity to do that right now. A very simple prayer of acceptance can be, "Lord Jesus, I believe in You. I want to receive You into my heart and life right now. I confess my sin; I ask forgiveness for that sin, and now I open the door of my heart and invite You to come in."

Why is the confession of sin so crucial to our knowing Jesus as Savior? It is sin that separates us from Him; in fact, "the wages of sin is death" (Romans 6:23). Sin lurks around every nook and cranny of our interior being, and in order to be free of it, we must confess it and then experience forgiveness of it. First John 1:9 (NKJV) tells us, "If we confess our sins, He is faithful and just to forgive us . . . all unrighteousness."

So then, we do not lose heavenly citizenship when we doubt. We lose heavenly citizenship when we reject God's offer of salvation through Christ. Those steps that Scripture outlines are profoundly simple. They offer us heaven.

"Help My Unbelief!"

But now let's talk about some faulty thinking concerning the role of doubt in a believer's life. A common assumption is that doubt is sin. That is not true. Doubt is sin only if it translates into an action that rejects God. Otherwise, doubt is to question the truth of something. Doubt is not *rejecting* truth; it is *questioning* truth. To doubt is to leave room for ultimate belief.

Is it possible for the Christian to doubt and still maintain heavenly citizenship? Of course. To be human is to at times doubt even the most basic elements of our faith. In fact, doubt can be an instrument for the building of faith.

> *Doubt is not rejecting truth; it is questioning truth.*
> *To doubt is to leave room for ultimate belief.*

Several chapters ago we discussed the exchange Jesus had with the father who sought healing for his son. In Mark 9:23–24 (NKJV), Jesus said to the father, "If you can believe, all things are possible to him who believes."

The boy's father responded to Jesus's call for belief with these words: "Lord, I believe; help my unbelief!"

That could be the life verse for all doubters. In other words, as the father did in answering Jesus, we can acknowledge that yes, we believe, but even so, there still are doubts. We can say, "Lord, help me with my doubts. There is room within me to experience greater belief, but my doubts sometimes threaten to swallow me up."

At one point during my health struggle with the consequences of silicone poisoning, I came to a place where my doubts threatened to swallow me up. That doubting experience was used as an instrument for the building of my faith. At the time, I did not feel the presence of God. I not only doubted His presence, I doubted His existence. This "dark night of the soul," as it was described by Saint John of the Cross, lasted only a few hours but was excruciating to me. My doubts in the past had been only minimal by comparison.

I was experiencing many physical impairments due to the silicone poisoning, which may have contributed to my spiritual vulnerability. Whatever the root cause, here's what happened.

I was sitting in a chair reading one of the psalms when I was overwhelmed with these thoughts: *This Christianity thing is total baloney. None of it is true. Why in the world am I sitting here reading from a book full of outlandish stories about a God who isn't real? Pick up a novel, Marilyn, and try to forget you're weak as a kitten, your muscles burn, and your brain keeps wandering off to la-la land, leaving you muddled.* With these thoughts, my interior world turned black. There was no light.

I sat there in that despairing state for about an hour. Then I began to mutter to myself, "Now wait a minute, Marilyn. There has to be a God. Only a God could make something out of nothing. How else do you explain the physical universe? It could not have simply 'big banged' itself into existence. That makes no sense.

"And then there's Jesus. History, both secular and Christian, supports the truth of His existence; you can't deny that, Marilyn. No well-informed person denies He lived and walked the earth. All one can do is deny He was God. But it does not make sense to deny He was God. Even non-Christian historians did not know how to account for His miracles. They did not deny them; they simply had no clue how to explain them.

"Then, of course, the clincher for me is the Resurrection. It is the examination of the resurrection story that has always inspired my faith in Jesus."

As I sat in my chair, still feeling the enveloping darkness shadow my soul, I began to go over those story facts piece by piece. I reminded myself that one of the best-supported facts surrounding the resurrection of Jesus is the empty tomb. There is solid, historical fact that the tomb of Jesus was empty on the original Easter morning.

The enemies of Jesus could have easily squashed Christianity by producing Christ's body. But they could not produce the body, so the Jewish religious leaders came up with a plan. The leaders bribed the guards to say they had fallen asleep at the tomb and that the apostles of Jesus had come during the night and stolen the body (see Matthew 28:11–15).

The holes in this story were as huge as Texas. How could

the apostles steal the body? They were devastated, heartbroken, and confused. They had thought Jesus was going to become their Jewish king, establish His kingdom on the earth, and liberate them all from the tyranny of the Roman Empire. But instead, He had been murdered. If He was God, why did He allow that? The only answer they could come up with was that He must not be God. They had made a mistake. They were all sitting on a pile of disillusionment.

Even if they did have the courage and motivation to steal the body, they would've had to get past the guards as well as move the large stone that sealed the tomb. But what would be their motivation for stealing the body? They had nothing to gain and everything to lose. Creating a hoax about Jesus's resurrection could only bring on ultimate persecution and possible death for their lie.

And if the apostles had stolen the body and created this huge lie about Jesus, why would they have been willing to die for what they knew was not even true? What would be the point?

Instead, the terrified and defeated apostles turned into courageous preachers and in some cases, martyrs. They became bold enough to stand against hostile Jews and Romans even in the face of torture and death.

What happened to cause them to believe as they did? They had seen the risen Jesus. In fact, numerous people (as many as five hundred) had encounters with Jesus after His resurrection. These witnesses claimed to have seen, heard, and touched Jesus. The world has never been the same.

This specific event in history, the resurrection of Jesus, started a movement that within four hundred years came to dominate the entire Roman Empire and, over the course of two thousand years, all of Western civilization.

> *As I recounted these resurrection facts to myself, the darkness started to lift. Light slowly filtered into my soul.*

As I sat there in my chair, I too began to sense the risen Christ. As I recounted these resurrection facts to myself, the darkness started to lift. Light slowly filtered into my soul. I knew that light was the light of the risen Christ. I was so grateful for the reemergence of my faith and the squashing of my doubt. I muttered to myself over and over again, "It's true. It's true. It's really, really true!"

My crisis of faith was a quiet and short-lived interior battle. But without it, I would not have known the drama of seeing the darkness flee from the force of that enveloping light. It wrapped itself around my troubled soul, and I began to feel restored.

Interestingly enough, it was not long after this experience that God began to heal my body of the poisons that had kept me nearly immobile for several months. Today I am still aware of the presence of silicone scattered about here and there in various organs, but I'm more aware of God's intentional resurrection power in my body. He's real. He's really, really real.

Doubts as Smoke Screens

Earlier I shared how I became a Christian at the age of five. This onslaught of doubt hit my spirit in my early sixties. Is it possible to have doubts and still be a Christian? Absolutely. I am here to testify to that reality. But there's a better way to live than to be mired in persistent doubt.

Let's go back to the women whose letters expressed doubts that were so strong they feared they might miss heaven.

One of the writers was bored with church, Bible study, and prayer. What's the problem there?

We all struggle with our humanity, which at times does not rise to the "faith occasion." Being distracted during church or chasing after our wandering minds during prayer is troubling but also human. If, however, distraction, lack of concentration, and indifference to the Spirit of God result in consistent doubt and boredom, there is a problem deeper than our vacillating humanity. Let's do some speculating about causes.

To begin with, it is common for people to throw up a few smoke screens to distract themselves from or cover up the real problem that is causing them to doubt. One of those root problems may be not wanting to lose personal control. An interior dialogue might sound like this: *I don't want God to get ahold of my life . . . I don't want to give up what I'm doing . . . He might want me to do something I don't want to do . . . I want to be in control . . . I can keep Him at arm's length by simply saying I have a lot of doubts . . . it doesn't make sense, and I can't help it—I'm bored.*

Another smoke screen may be based on anger at God and what He has allowed to happen. This was the case in my other doubting correspondent. It may be easier for her to blame away her lack of spiritual contentment to problems with doubt instead of owning up to her problems of resentment with God.

Facing God in her vulnerability would mean she would have to respond to the force of His love. Perhaps she no longer trusts that love and does not want to risk trusting it again. It's easier to just remain a doubter. Less is required . . . it's safer.

Now let's take a step back and speculate on what in their backgrounds may have resulted in these women's troubling doubts. Unfortunately, parents often shape our ideas about who God is, how He behaves, and what He expects of us. If these women have a parent who gave little room for failure, it may be frightening to attempt a relationship with God. They may fear disappointing Him by their inability to "do it right." It's easier to be a doubter than to risk His not being pleased with them.

The first woman may also have a temperament prone to melancholy. It's difficult to have a happy faith experience when nothing in life makes a lot of sense or even holds much promise for meaning. For a melancholy temperament, faith is not the only challenge; sometimes life itself is.

Both women may insist that if all their doubts and questions are not answered satisfactorily, there is no choice but to remain a doubter. They can't enter into a faith-walk unless there are no questions. They must have proof in order to believe. They must have proof before they can clear out the doubts.

All these smoke screens boil down to one basic emotion: fear.

- Fear that God will take away personal control.

- Fear that God might melt the anger barrier.

- Fear that God may find a less-than-perfect-performance person.

- Fear about everything, believing life is hard.

- Fear that God doesn't have the answers for doubt.

A Matter of the Will

The absence of fear does not mean doubt disappears. But facing those fears and realizing they are smoke screens to faith is a positive step in the direction of moving from doubt to faith. Actually, for those of us who don't relinquish control easily, here's a comforting thought: Faith can be a matter of the will. I can will to believe, or I can will to not believe. The choice is mine. That means I can choose to live with faith rather than fear.

Faith can be a matter of the will. I can will to believe, or I can will to not believe. The choice is mine. That means I can choose to live with faith rather than fear.

John 7:12–17 (NKJV) describes an interesting incident in which Jesus talked about the strength of the will:

There was much complaining among the people concerning Him. Some said, "He is good"; others said, "No, on the contrary, He deceives the people." However, no one spoke openly of Him for fear of the Jews. . . .

The Jews marveled, saying, "How does this Man know letters, having never studied?" Jesus answered them and said, "My doctrine is not Mine, but His who sent Me. If anyone wills to do His will, he shall know concerning the doctrine."

Jesus encouraged the unbelievers who were surrounding Him in the temple that they could "[will] to do His will." If they did, they would know who authored the doctrine about which Jesus spoke. He was encouraging them to a place of personal willingness.

John 12:37 (NKJV) also records a revealing incident regarding the will as it related to the many miracles Jesus performed before the people. It says, "Although He had done so many signs before them, they did not believe in Him."

Despite the miraculous visual witness of God's power, there were many who simply willed against what they saw and what they had no explanation for. They chose not to believe. They were not even doubters; they were unbelievers. The doubter leaves room to be convinced of truth. The unbeliever turns from truth.

Several weeks ago my heart was touched by a doubter. There was room in her heart for truth; she did not turn away in disbelief. The occasion for this experience was with a newspaper reporter assigned by her editor to cover our Women of Faith conference in their city. She was to interview me during one of our Saturday morning breaks. She came to the interview with a look of total disinterest. She had no desire to talk to me and even less desire to cover something with the corny title "Women of Faith."

After a few preliminary questions, she looked me straight in the eye and said, "Can you prove absolutely the existence of God?"

I looked into her gray eyes and said, "No . . . I cannot absolutely prove the existence of God. But there's enough evidence in favor of believing in His existence to tilt me into the camp of faith."

She put her pen down for a moment and stared at me. Then she said, "You really believe it, don't you?"

"With all my heart," I responded.

She softened; we talked.

She had come in to do a quick interview, write the story, and be gone. Instead, she stayed for the rest of the day. Her spirit was moved. She wrote an enthusiastic story that made it onto the front page of her large and influential paper. Faith was making moves on her.

You may be one upon whom faith is making moves. Your doubts have caused you to cry out. Your back is against the wall, but remember, while you are there, at your wits' end, God shares the wall with you. Psalm 94:19 is a tender reminder of God's love for the doubter: "When doubts filled my mind, your comfort gave me renewed hope and cheer."

This book is primarily about faith. That may be a difficult topic for those of you who struggle with doubt. I'd like to make a few suggestions that may contribute to your "renewed hope and cheer":

- Be assured that you do not lose your heavenly citizenship when you doubt.

- Make a conscious decision about your doubt: do you will to believe? If so, you will need the Author of your belief to help you. Say to Him, "I will to believe. Help me with my will. Please strengthen it, focus it, enable it to do what I can't do in my human weakness."

- Study the object of your faith. Read the Gospel of John over and over and over again. (I suggest that Gospel because it has the greatest number of Jesus quotes.)

- Get involved in a Bible study where you are safe and will not receive gasps and groans when you honestly share your doubts.

- Keep a prayer journal. Write your prayers to God. Then read your prayers out loud to Him. This will help you corral your mind and your concentration when you talk to Him.

- Go to church. Jesus went to church, and I can't imagine how He kept from being bored. After all, He knew more than anyone there! But He went to worship. There is a sweet spirit of worship that settles over the soul when we all come together for that purpose. If the sermon is a challenge to your attention, take notes. It will help you remain focused. If the sermon cannot be outlined and has no sequential flow, perhaps your pastor should take English Comp 101. (Forget you read that last sentence.)

Finally, let me say for those of you who want all your questions answered, that day will never come this side of eternity. The sixteenth-century mystic Madam Jeanne Guyon wrote:

If knowing answers to life's questions is absolutely necessary to you, then forget about the journey. You will never make it, for this is a journey of unknowables—of unanswered questions, enigmas, incomprehensibles, and most of all, things unfair.

Our challenge is to love Him for what we do see and trust Him for what we cannot see. Rising to that challenge may prevent us from tailgating or losing our tempers when the law-abiding driver ahead of us stops at a yellow light. Our doubts may occasionally persist, but they do not have to dictate our behavior. It's more fun when faith does that.

1. Do you think a person who struggles with doubt is really a Christian?

2. Do you think doubt is a sin? Can you say that you don't doubt God is real, that Jesus is your Savior, and heaven is a real place?

3. Talk about a specific time of doubt in your life. How was your faith restored?

Wits' end is no place for laughter

Have you heard of "letterboxing"? It has become a near obsession in the United States. It got its start in England 150 years ago when a fellow out for his morning walk left a bottle by Cranmere Pool with his calling card in it. He invited anyone who found the hidden bottle to add his/her calling card to the bottle and hide it in a new location.

The British hide-and-seek game caught on here after an article appeared in *Smithsonian* magazine in 1998. Since that article was published, more than nine thousand letterboxes (no bottles) have been planted in state parks and nature preserves around the country.

The letterbox now contains a logbook and a rubber stamp. When the carefully hidden letterbox is found, the finder marks the logbook with his or her own personal stamp to document the discovery. Great secrecy is used in rehiding the letterbox, and clues to its new location are posted on a letterboxing Web site. *Time* magazine reported that the number of hits on the site doubled recently from 206,513 in May 2003 to more than half a million in April 2004.

What's the appeal? Apparently it's considered a good old-fashioned puzzle—a treasure hunt. There is the challenge of leaving creative clues on the Web site and then placing the boxes in ingenious locations. This can inspire the imaginations of an entire family as they join together in a weekend box search.

Searching Out God's Gift of Humor in Unexpected Places

The "searching for clues" mentality undoubtedly characterizes many of us as we puzzle through Scripture in an effort to find God's truth, especially when we're spending wits'-end time with our backs against the wall. We tend to think there's no possible place for humor as we cry out to God and wait for Him to deliver us. But that's faulty thinking. In fact, humor can be a great source of strength and encouragement during our wits'-end wall-waiting time. I thought of that fact as I read about the phenomenon of the letterboxing craze. It helped me see how our search for God's sovereign will and His purpose in our trip to the wall can be a benefit in itself, inspiring us to find hidden rewards in the experiences we've been called to endure. Those rewards—or that deliverance—may be different from the way we imagined them. And one of those hidden treasures we find during our search might be the gift of humor God may have left for us in un-expected places . . . even places like that wits'-end wall.

> *We tend to think there's no possible place*
> *for humor as we cry out to God and wait for Him*
> *to deliver us. But that's faulty thinking.*

The Bible frequently speaks of searching and of the reward to those who seek spiritual truth found only in God:

- Psalm 69:32 (NKJV): "You who seek God, your hearts shall live."

- Isaiah 58:2 (NIV): "Day after day they seek me out; they seem eager to know my ways."

- Proverbs 28:5 (NIV): "Evil men do not understand justice, but those who seek the LORD understand it fully."

- Matthew 7:7–8 (NIV): "Ask and it will be given to you; seek and you will find; knock and the door will be opened to you. For everyone who asks receives; he who seeks finds; and to him who knocks, the door will be opened."

- Hebrews 11:6 (NKJV): "He is a rewarder of those who diligently seek Him."

There is encouragement to those of us who are eager to know God's ways: His Word promises that we are indeed rewarded as we "diligently seek Him." But we've also talked about God as a mystery whose "ways [are] past finding out" (Romans 11:33 NKJV), as well as the fact that His ways are not our ways (see Isaiah 55:8). I must content myself with that element of God's mystery. I will never fully understand or know all there is to know about who He is, what He does, and why He does it.

But God is not the only mystery in life. I don't understand electricity, wind currents, molecular theory, or computers either. Sometimes I feel an affinity for the mental challenge Farmer Brown experienced in differentiating his two horses. The only way he could tell them apart was that the black one was an inch taller than the white one.

Can we reduce God to black or white? No. But one of the purposes of this book is to pick up the clues we can find in Scripture that will help those of us who find wits' end a frequent mailing address.

A Different Means of Deliverance

We started with the promise in Psalm 107:28 that tells us when we "cry out" to God, He delivers us from our "distresses." What we do not know is how or when He delivers. We assume, as well as hope, His deliverance means a change in our circumstances. We want to see that deliverance!

There's an old Gaelic blessing that gives me a giggle:

May those who love us, love us.
And those that don't love us
May God turn their hearts:
And if He does not turn their hearts,
may He turn their ankles
So we'll know them by their limping.

As much as we would like to see a change of circumstances as evidence that God is delivering us from our distresses, often our circumstances do not change. Then how can God promise He will deliver us from our distresses? Is there a little clause somewhere that we missed? Is it written in invisible ink?

I believe God always delivers us from our distresses just as He promised, but sometimes that deliverance is within our hearts, where the pain of our circumstances has shredded our interior being. God meets us at the shredding place. His deliverance may be simply to give us comfort in that place. His deliverance may be a lifting of our heads . . . of our spirits . . . and an assurance that He is there with us. His deliverance may be giving us the knowledge that we will have His strength to endure even though our circumstances may not change.

> *God always delivers us from our distresses just as He promised, but sometimes that deliverance is within our hearts, where the pain of our circumstances has shredded our interior being. God meets us at the shredding place.*

If, indeed, that is God's means of deliverance, how we choose to react to that kind of deliverance is crucial to our peace. If we say, "Sorry, God, that's a cop-out. You said *deliverance*. I want things to change. I want the real deal, not this heart-comfort thing. Deliverance means You fix it. I'm waiting for that, and until I get it, I'm going to think You're taking the easy way out of your promise."

How we think determines how we feel. The mind is able to exert a tremendous influence over our emotions and bodies. If our responses to God are negative, angry, and resentful, we're going to find our time at the wits'-end wall utterly miserable. We may even become physically sick as our thoughts spiral downward and a sense of helplessness washes over us.

On the other hand, if we are enabled to embrace God's method of deliverance, which may be to lift our heads and hearts and see Him at the wall as a loving presence whose intent is to strengthen us and not desert us, we then will avoid the misery and bitterness of negative, faith-challenged thinking. We have a choice in how we respond to the wall.

A Method That Works Every Time

I've been at that wall. I've wondered about God's promise to deliver, and I've tried to seek out answers to the dilemmas I've faced. In the wall-waiting, searching time, I've learned something very valuable about how to do that waiting. It's a method that joins forces with my will to believe God is working on my behalf and affirms the fact that God is sharing the wall with me. (Remember, He is wherever we are. If we're at the wall, He is too.)

The method? Humor. It works every time. I stumbled onto this method when I was nine years old. In an earlier chapter I described the desolation I felt at Dad's "Lonely Acres," during the time that was meant to restore his health and vitality but in the process nearly destroyed mine. One afternoon I was reading my *Playmate* magazine and came across a joke I found hysterically funny. I thought most of the jokes in *Playmate* were dumb, but this one tickled me to the very core of my being. It was too good for only one reading, so I read it repeatedly, laughed each time, and quickly memorized it. (I'm sorry to say, all these decades later, I have forgotten the joke. But I still remember the humorous lift it gave me.)

That night, having gone to bed and hearing the usual but unsettling howl of coyotes, I decided to tell myself the great joke I'd memorized that afternoon. The familiarity of the joke had not diminished its laughter-producing effect. When I laughed audibly, both parents rushed to my bedroom to check my well-being. I was still laughing when they snapped on the light. When I shared the source of my giggles and why I had recited it to myself, their spontaneous laughter assured me it truly *was* a great joke. We then had a chat about coyotes and what they might do when they quit howling. Were they known to come out of the hills and peer into the windows of unsuspecting people? If so, might they "break and enter"? How did they feel about children?

> *Laughter serves a greater purpose than*
> *just distracting us from our misery as we do our*
> *time at the wall. It's good medicine.*

The coyotes had become a minor wits'-end experience for me, but I'd found a perfect antidote for their mournful yet threatening howls: I told myself a joke. I added other jokes to my prize *Playmate* joke and soon had at least ten minutes' worth of good jokes that, to some degree, distracted me from my concerns about the intentions and whereabouts of the coyotes.

Laughter serves a greater purpose than just distracting us from our misery as we do our time at the wall. It's good medicine. Proverbs 17:22 (NKJV) states, "A merry heart does good, like medicine, but a broken spirit dries the bones." You are undoubtedly aware of the modern medical research supporting Solomon's wisdom declaring laughter to be good medicine. We now know laughter releases the brain's natural painkillers, endorphins, which can be fifty times more powerful than morphine. Laughter not only reduces pain, it lowers blood pressure and relaxes the skeletal frame. A good laugh may drive us to our knees simply because the skeletal frame can no longer hold us up. (Some prefer that to prayer.)

One morning as Ken took his place in the lineup of chairs occupied by cancer patients getting their chemo drips, he was startled from his reading by the continual eruptions of laughter coming from the woman sitting next to him. She was obviously getting a kick out of her book. Ken leaned over in an attempt to see the cover. To his great pleasure, she was reading my first book, *Choosing the Amusing.*

He poked her gently and said, "I know the author of that book."

Without looking up, she said, "The author's wonderfully crazy."

Ken responded, "That's why I married her. She needed my help."

Still without looking up, the reader said, "She's helping me. I feel so much better; she really makes me laugh."

Ken's response: "Me too."

The woman never looked up. I like to think she couldn't tear herself away from the pages for even a second.

This dear lady was finding humor to be a great method of dealing with her wits'-end cancer. Ken used it for his cancer wits'-enders as well. At one point he had lost more than one hundred pounds and was not expected to live more than a few more days. But God wasn't ready for him; Ken rallied and began to gain weight and felt well enough to work part-time for Chuck Swindoll's *Insight for Living* ministry.

For that Ken needed a new suit. In his existing suits, he could twirl around without causing the garments to move. So he went to a tailor for a personally fitted suit that would accommodate his new lithe body. When Ken told the tailor that the loss of one hundred pounds made the new suit necessary, the tailor was envious. "You know," he said, "I'd like to take off at least fifty pounds. What's your secret?"

"Cancer," Ken said wryly.

After a brief silence, the tailor picked up on Ken's black humor and said, "That's a bit severe. Maybe I'll just get my stomach stapled . . . got a lot of staples right here in the shop."

As difficult as Ken's cancer and resulting death were for me to bear, I am grateful for the gifts of humor he left behind during that time we spent with our backs against the wall, waiting for God's deliverance. It was a tender time for us but also a period of stress.

Shortly before he died, I told Ken that I was going to stop bothering to color my hair. It was an unnecessary hassle that I wanted to forgo as I helped him during his declining health. I'd been coloring it for a thousand years and had always thought I should just let it go gray, but Ken hadn't wanted me to.

Now I told him, "There's no point in continuing to color it. You're not going to be here to notice."

"Wait a minute, Marilyn," he told me. "I know how you can get a lot of mileage out of this."

"Mileage! What are you talking about?" I asked him.

"How long will it take to grow out your hair?"

"I don't know. I have no idea what's under there," I answered. "About three months, I guess. Why?" I was totally perplexed by the scheme he seemed to be hatching.

"OK, Marilyn, here's what you do: After my funeral,

don't go out for three months, until your hair's grown out. You see, everyone will see you at the service, and they'll see your hair looking as it normally does. Then, when you go out three months later and your hair is gray, they'll be shocked. They'll say, 'Oh, poor Marilyn! She's grieving so deeply for her dear Ken that her hair has gone completely gray. We have to help her, poor thing.' They'll be falling all over themselves to take you to dinner and the movies and to bring you presents. I'm telling you, Marilyn, you'll get a lot of mileage out of this."

The Value of Humor during Wits'-End Times

This experience—and many others—has taught me the value of using humor during wits'-end times. There's no end to the health-producing effects we experience from laughter. In fact, laughter often precedes trust. When I laugh, I am in essence saying to God, "I trust You, even though I'm not sure what You're doing." A verse from *The Message* translation of the Bible brings these thoughts together beautifully:

You never saw him, yet you love him. You still don't see him, yet you trust him—with laughter and singing. (1 Peter 1:8 MSG)

When I'm trusting Him during my wits'-end wall-wait, laughter opens the door, not only to trusting, but to an inspired tendency toward singing His praises. As Psalm 104:33 (NKJV) says,

I will sing to the LORD as long as I live;
I will sing praise to my God while I have my being.

In our laughing, we relax in His promised care; in our trusting we believe Him for what we don't see, and in our singing we praise Him for who He is.

These techniques for wits'-end living are not buried in a bottle in an obscure location. They're found in our faith object: the Bible, God's Word. His promise is that when we seek, we will find. Laughing and singing facilitate the search for all truth anywhere, anytime.

1. What makes you laugh? Have you ever thought to use laughter as one way to live through your wits'-end experiences? Discuss a time when laughter gave you a little break from your wall-wait.

2. Why do you suppose God thinks so highly of laughter? There are God-oriented benefits from laughter. What are they? God obviously laughs or He would not have created us with that capacity. Search out a good laugh today and share it with someone.

The Wrap-Up:
I think I'm getting it!
(Preparing for that next wits'-end experience)

There are three major review points I want to chat about as we wrap up what we've learned concerning God at our wits' end:

1. Bad things are not happening to us because God is punishing us for confessed and forgiven sin.

2. Faith is God's gift to us, and all the human effort and calisthenics in the world will not beef it up.

3. God is not just a trifle sovereign. He is fully sovereign, which means He rules.

One of the most liberating truths we find in Scripture is that bad things happening to us are not God's punishment for sin. Isaiah 13:11 (NKJV)—"I will punish the world for its evil, and the wicked for their iniquity"—was written for those who never sought forgiveness from the God who freely forgives and thoroughly cleanses us from the stain of our sins. He tenderly says to us, "I write to you, little children, because your sins are forgiven you for His name's sake" (1 John 2:12 NKJV).

Whose name's sake? Jesus's. He paid the price for our sins.

We need always to keep in mind the distinction between consequences of sin and punishment for sin. Punishment for sin, death, has already taken place. That occurred at the cross. But consequences of our sins may go on for a lifetime. Those consequences may be felt in our daily lives. For example, drugs, alcohol, or sexual addictions leave their mark upon our bodies as well as upon our psyches. But the good news is, whatever was the sin that held us in its grip is forgiven. We can look at the consequences as reminders of God's grace and love for us. He is not holding that sin against us but is encouraging us to move on with our lives and enjoy the grace of His forgiveness.

> *We can look at the consequences as*
> *reminders of God's grace and love for us.*

Another crucial clue for understanding our lives with God is to realize that faith is His gift to us. We can't scrunch it into existence. Jesus is the "author and finisher of our faith" (Hebrews 12:2 NKJV). We received that gift when we received Him into our hearts and lives for salvation. With salvation came faith to believe. Without faith, we would not have it in our hearts to receive Jesus in the first place. In our natural selves, we would be indifferent to the spiritual light, which is Jesus. Why? The sinner prefers darkness. So no one who knows Christ can say, "I have no faith." Faith is part of the salvation package.

All faith, no matter how poor or weak, serves as our conduit . . . our contact to the source of our faith, who is Christ Jesus. Many of us fear our faith is too small, too feeble to be effective for our lives. We must remember that no matter how small our faith may be, it is connected to Him who is not small or feeble. He authors our faith, so we know it's there. Jesus says even if it's as small as a mustard seed, it is still powerful. Why? Because that faith is authored by Him.

There are choices we can make about our faith. We can will in our spirits to grow, develop, and mature in that God-given faith. Or we can choose to hang back and hold on to the human thing that wills us not to get too involved. We fear it might require too much of us. We can choose to remain babies in our faith-growth and not develop past the Gerber-strained-foods stage. But keep in mind, Hebrews 5:12–14 does a bit of scolding for those who will themselves into a place of permanent spiritual infancy:

> Though by this time you ought to be teachers, you need someone to teach you again the first principles of the oracles of God; and you have come to need milk and not solid food. For everyone who partakes only of milk is unskilled in the word of righteousness, for he is a babe. But solid food belongs to those who are of full age. (NKJV)

What we want to remember about the growing of our faith is that our "food" is found in Scripture. We don't even have to dash to Albertson's market each week to stock up. Everything we need for healthy faith-growth is in the Bible. We may eat all we can hold and not gain weight. If you supplement with chocolate . . . that's your choice.

Finally, I remind you of God's sovereignty. Remember, He is not just a little bit sovereign; He is utterly and completely sovereign. What does that mean? He controls everything. Not just some things . . . *everything*. Does He control our sins? He does not ordain or initiate sin, but He is in control of the aftermath of sin. Plain and simple: He rules.

The perfect example of how God is in control of the aftermath of sin is what happened in the Garden of Eden. From that sin of disobedience came the plan of God to make provision for the removal of sin from His creation through Jesus Christ.

There is a settled peace deep within my soul as I realize I am not in charge of my life. I'm responsible to that life, but I don't have the power to orchestrate the events in my life any more than I have the power to make the moon appear twice every month instead of once. What I can do is enter into a partnership with God about my life.

In that partnership I'm given a major clue about how that partnership works. Ephesians 1:11 (NKJV) says He "works all things according to the counsel of His will." I put myself in a place of willing acceptance of His sovereign design . . . of His will.

The mystery to me is that He invites my participation in the living out of that design. I'm not quite sure what that means or how much latitude I have as I partner with Him. But I do know I'm to daily seek His guidance and wisdom. I also know I'm to conscientiously live my days according to the practical principles He has laid out for me in Scripture.

God's sovereignty will always hold levels of mystery for me, but that mystery need never interfere with my peace. In fact, God's mystery feeds my peace. Why? Because I have faith in Him. He has a good track record. I like it that He knows more than I do. I also like His style. He's creative, has a flair, and does the unexpected. But coupled with that drama and flair are His tender love and regard for me. When I have veered off the path through a willful disregard for what I know to be wise, He reassures me of His care.

There you have it: the strong, tender love of a sovereign God

Who redeems your life from destruction,
Who crowns you with lovingkindness and tender mercies.
(Psalm 103:4 NKJV)

Can't beat that.

Preparing for the Next Trip to the Wall

As we anticipate our next wits'-end experience (we all will have them until we're escorted off this earth), we want to pay attention to what we believe and what we think about the wits'-end experience itself. Hopefully we've internalized the biblical fact that we are not being punished because of sin. Whether or not we believe we are, our thinking will reflect that belief. But if we're thinking, *What did I do to bring this on? What sin has caught up with me?* our thinking is faulty. We want to remind ourselves of the difference between the consequence of sin, which is the human spillover, and the sin itself. The sin itself, once confessed, is forgiven. If we believe that, we'll stop rifling through our mental files trying to pinpoint the sin-cause of our wits'-end experiences.

Let's swing back now to the Hedrick Racing Pigs who raced one another for the prize of one Oreo cookie. The pigs believed in the existence of the cookie because they could see it. But if Snoop Hoggy Hog made it to the finish line first for weeks at a time, I suggested that Arnold Snoutzenhogger and his other three racing buddies might sink to the dirt in discouragement and never race again. Why? Because they could not actually see the prize. If they could not see it, they no longer believed in its existence.

We want to remember that faith goes beyond belief. Belief is mental acceptance. Faith is mental acceptance coupled with spiritual enablement to embrace what we cannot see. Faith would mean the pigs ran whether or not they saw the cookie. Many of us identify with the discouragement of the pigs when they lost sight of the prize. We want to see in order to have faith. It's easier that way. Seeing feeds the emergence of faith, which is why Jesus performed miracles. But the true test of our faith is when faith exists without visible proof.

Remember Thomas? Thomas is the most famous doubter on record. He was a disciple of Jesus who saw miracles only Jesus could do. But in spite of all Thomas had seen that should have translated from belief to faith, after the Crucifixion Thomas lost his faith. Why? What he saw did not make sense. Jesus died on a cross. Jesus was supposed to become the earthly ruler for the Jews and stamp out the injustice and tyranny of the Roman Empire. Thomas was doing some faulty thinking that eroded his faith. Jesus had told the disciples His kingdom would not yet be on this earth. But that was not what Thomas wanted to believe, so he rejected it all.

When the other disciples saw Jesus after the Resurrection and excitedly told Thomas about it, his response was, "Unless I see in His hands the print of the nails, and put my finger into the print of the nails, and put my hand into His side, I will not believe" (John 20:25 NKJV).

Eight days after this statement, "Jesus came, the doors being shut, and stood in the midst, and said, 'Peace to you!' Then He said to Thomas, 'Reach your finger here, and look at My hands; and reach your hand here, and put it into My side'" (John 20:26–27 NKJV).

Jesus scolded Thomas a bit then, saying, "Do not be unbelieving, but believing. . . . Because you have seen Me, you have believed. Blessed are those who have not seen and yet have believed" (John 20:27–29 NKJV).

These statements make us shrink back into old thinking that says, *I've got to beef up my faith because if I don't, Jesus has reason to scold me.* What is touching to me about how Jesus dealt with Thomas is that Jesus met Thomas at the place of his unbelief. Thomas needed to see, so Jesus showed him the marks on His body. Thomas was satisfied and believed. At that point, his belief was mental assent, but my guess is it translated quickly into faith.

We all need encouragement to raise the level of our faith from seeing to trusting. But we must remember that the author of our faith is Jesus. He meets us at our level of need, as He did Thomas. Thomas was at rock bottom; he had hit the wall. Jesus went there with him. When you and I are at rock bottom, when our backs are to the wall in a wits'-end experience, Jesus will meet us there. Remember the doubter's prayer: "I believe; help my unbelief." Faulty thinking would be to think your faith development is your job and you'd better get on the ball! Faith thinking is trusting God to give you what you can't produce apart from Him.

In anticipation of a few more wits'-enders, my prayer is that we all will avoid faulty thinking and shaky faith. Ecclesiastes 7:14 (NKJV) puts our life experiences in a nutshell:

In the day of prosperity be joyful,
But in the day of adversity consider:
Surely God has appointed the one as well as the other.

I choose to joyfully live out those days of prosperity and trust His sovereign design for those days of adversity.

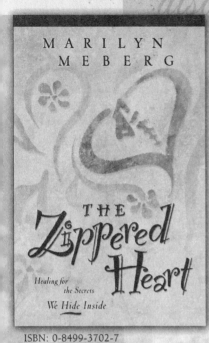

MARILYN
MEBERG

THE
Zippered
Heart

*Healing for
the Secrets*
We Hide Inside

ISBN: 0-8499-3702-7

In *The Zippered Heart*, Marilyn does a gentle exploration of those secrets and issues which, if denied, can rob us of the abundant life we are promised in Christ. God means for us to be whole. This book is an encouragement in that process.

"This book will change lives, because it requires that we look precisely at both the dark and the light sides of ourselves. Then it brings an over-flowing grace and forgiveness. As a psychologist with thirty-five years of clinical experience, I can say that this is one of the best books I have read."

—NEAL CLARK WARREN

"For thirty years Marilyn's compassionate exploration of the human heart has amazed me. Now, with skill and tenderness she opens that heart for all of us to see how fearfully and wonderfully we are made."

—LUCI SWINDOLL

"*The Zippered Heart* is a perceptive and sensitive examination of the 'war within' between our two natures."

—ARCHIBALD D. HART, PH.D.

W PUBLISHING GROUP
A Division of Thomas Nelson Publishers
Since 1798

For other life-changing resources, visit us at:
www.thomasnelson.com

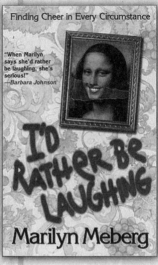

Finding Cheer in Every Circumstance

"When Marilyn says she'd rather be laughing, she's serious!"
—Barbara Johnson

Marilyn Meberg

0-8499-3989-5

also available

Heartbreaking losses can steal the cheer from anyone's life. But there's a way to overcome the tribulations that threaten your happiness and shadow your days. In this clever and inspirational book, experienced counselor and popular speaker Marilyn Meberg shows you how to triumph and choose to laugh instead of cry.

With warm encouragement, contagious enthusiasm, and a dash of mischievous humor, she shares the powerful medicine of God's Word. As the light of His love courses through your heart, you'll soon find yourself agreeing: *I'd Rather Be Laughing!*

"When Marilyn Meberg says she'd rather be laughing, she's serious! This book is a carbonated taste of Jesus' Good News message. It bubbles with enthusiasm, sparkles with fun, and inspires readers to overcome life's problems with the God-given gift of laughter. I loved it!"

—BARBARA JOHNSON

W PUBLISHING GROUP
A Division of Thomas Nelson Publishers
Since 1798

For other life-changing resources, visit us at:
www.thomasnelson.com

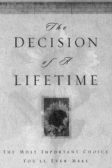

THE DECISION OF A LIFETIME
(0-8499-4420-1)

How will you respond to an offer of perfect love?

The Creator God has chosen you. In His mind, there is no questioning your value: You are His masterpiece, His special treasure. It's not a goal you strive to achieve, a reward you try to earn, or a status you struggle to deserve. Quite simply, God loves you just as you are, and He wants to adopt you.

But unlike most adoptions, you have a choice in deciding whether you want to be adopted. With humor and insight, popular speaker and author Marilyn Meberg lays out the facts to help you make this all-important choice.

How will you respond to God's offer of love, salvation, and personal adoption?

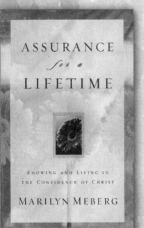

ASSURANCE FOR A LIFETIME
(0-8499-4500-3)

You accepted Jesus as your personal Savior. But it all seemed so easy. Maybe now you're questioning whether you're really a Christian. And perhaps you're wondering, *What do I do now?*

Using the same insight, enthusiasm, and humor that touched thousands of lives in her best-selling book *The Decision of a Lifetime,* gifted Bible teacher and popular author Marilyn Meberg launches you on the next step of your Christian walk with this book.

In *Assurance of a Lifetime,* you'll learn how to claim the absolute assurance of Christ's love for you, to accept His total forgiveness of your sins, and to tap into the power of the Holy Spirit and let God work His wonders in your life.

W PUBLISHING GROUP
A Division of Thomas Nelson Publishers
Since 1798